Language Research in the Impact of Aging Through Transitivity

The Case of Chinese Elders' Narratives

年龄因素的及物性研究

——以中国老年人叙述为例

徐兴仁 著

南开大学出版社

天 津

图书在版编目(CIP)数据

年龄因素的及物性研究：以中国老年人叙述为例：
英文／徐兴仁著. —天津：南开大学出版社，2018.12
ISBN 978-7-310-05698-9

Ⅰ.①年… Ⅱ.①徐… Ⅲ.①老年人－应用语言学－
研究－英文 Ⅳ.①H08

中国版本图书馆 CIP 数据核字(2018)第 272589 号

南开大学出版社出版发行
出版人：刘运峰
地址：天津市南开区卫津路 94 号　　　邮政编码：300071
营销部电话：(022)23508339　23500755
营销部传真：(022)23508542　　　邮购部电话：(022)23502200

*

北京建宏印刷有限公司印刷
全国各地新华书店经销

*

2018 年 12 月第 1 版　　2018 年 12 月第 1 次印刷
230×155 毫米　16 开本　10 印张　152 千字
定价：40.00 元

如遇图书印装质量问题,请与本社营销部联系调换,电话：(022)23507125

前　言

本书系作者在美国宾夕法尼亚州立大学应用语言学系攻读博士学位时期的毕业论文，后在该论文的基础上精心修改而成。作者应用及物性探索年龄因素对语言能力的影响，提出了一种应用系统功能语言学研究中国老年人叙事能力的新方法，并提出了新的结论，反映了该领域研究的最新成果。

专家学者们在研究叙事语言能力与年龄的关系时大多采用著名神经语言学家帕拉底（Paradis）的叙事测试工具。然而，这一叙事测试工具在实际操作中存在着缺陷，测试角度不够宽广，未能真实地反映被测试者叙事语言能力。本人在马考尼（Makoni）教授的指导下，对这一叙事测试工具进行了修改，并且应用了韩礼德（Halliday）系统功能语言学的及物（transitivity）理论，建立了一种新的测试工具，创造性地使用了统计学计算方法，证实了作者提出的被测试者叙事的语言能力与年龄发展的不均衡性的设想，对该领域的研究做出了重要的贡献。

本人非常感谢曾经支持和帮助我从事这项研究的专家和学者们。他们是马考尼（Sinfree B. Makoni）教授（我的导师和答辩委员会主席）、萨维尼翁（Sandra J. Savignon）教授、陆（Xiaofei Lu）教授、游（Xiaoye You）教授，以及宾夕法尼亚州立大学应用语言学系主任霍尔（Joan Kelly Hall）教授、语言习得中心主任兰托夫（James P. Lantolf）教授，荷兰格罗宁根（Groningen）大学应用语言学系主任、教授博特（Kees de Bot）等。本书的出版得到了河北工业大学外国语学院院长史耕山教授的鼓励和支持，在此表示感谢。欢迎专家学者提出宝贵意见。

ABSTRACT

The research applies transitivity of Systemic Functional Theory (SFT) to examine age impact on picture-elicited narratives of elderly Chinese participants. The choice of using SFT is that SFT studies language through "context of situation" and reveals meaning potential in the context. Transitivity of SFT is compatible with Chinese language, and it provides a solution to the problem raised by Makoni, Lin and Schrauf who argue that the analysis is complicated because it is difficult to use Western views when analyzing Chinese texts. Transitivity and its six processes uncover subtle aspects of participants' performances in picture-elicited narratives, and thus they provide a detailed understanding of age impact which cannot be obtained otherwise. The research uses 60 Chinese participants whose age range is from 50 to 79 years old. The participants are equally divided into three age groups: A (50-59 years old), B (60-69 years old) and C (70-79 years old) with 10 males and 10 females in each group. The elicited narratives are secondary data from Paradis. In the present research, the narratives are encoded by two separate raters according to the coding system developed by the author who gives a great consideration to Paradis' stimuli and the six processes of transitivity. The present study uses General Linear Model in ANOVA to analyze the encoded data to find age impact on the participants' transitivity performances so that the participants' factors, levels and the interactions of factors and levels are taken into account. The results indicate that age can statistically have a significant impact on the participants' transitivity performances. The points of the participants' performances increased from Group A to Group B, and the points of participants' performances decreased from Group B to Group C. Education and gender do not have a significant impact. The significance of the present study is that it reveals the age impact on participants' transitivity performances in detail, and that it revises the previous researchers' general assertion. Finally the author critically evaluates the strength and limitation of the present and suggests directions for future research.

TABLE OF CONTENTS

LIST OF TABLES

LIST OF FIGURES

ACKNOWLEDGEMENTS

I would like to express my greatest gratitude to Sinfree B. Makoni, my mentor and my adviser, who suggested my research direction at a very early time when I began to know him. He has been always ready to help and find answers to my questions with wisdom and professional sharpness in the academic field. He has provided me with a lot of valuable advice during my study and research, and he has undertaken the tremendous hard work of reading my papers and the drafts of dissertation and suggested the ways for improvement.

I would also like to express my deepest gratitude to Sandra J. Savignon, my mentor, who provided a lot of valuable advice and help both in academic study and in my life. She is an outstanding international scholar, and she is ready to help when I need help. I have learned many things from her in second language acquisition, communicative language teaching and systemic functional linguistics.

I would give my heartfelt thanks to Xiaofei Lu, who has spent lot time in reading my drafts and provided me with valuable advice for improvement. He has always been ready to help in a very professional way and in a timely manner when I have questions and need his help.

I would also give my heartfelt thanks to Xiaoye You, who provided valuable suggestions in literature review. He inspired my critical thinking, and encouraged me to give a critical review on the previous research in the field. I thank him for the lot of time he spent in reading my drafts and for his creative feedbacks.

Chapter 1   INTRODUCTION

1.1 Background

Language is of great importance in studying aging and aging-related areas such as neurology and gerontology because of the role it has played in the following four aspects. First, language can be used as a window to understand the brain function (Goodglass and Kaplan 1983; Melrose 2005); second, the ability of using language can contribute to our understanding of the status of normal people (defined as the people who have no history of neurological or psychiatric illness, or other problems) (Armstrong 2005); third, language can be used for the facilitation and treatment of the aphasic patients (Armstrong 2005); fourth, language can be used to understand the social functions and status of the elders (Makoni 1997, 2001, 2002). The present research belongs to the second aspect in the above, and it will explore in depth how age can have an impact on the normal elders' language ability in the picture-elicited narratives. Specifically, the present research will explore how age can have an impact on the use of transitivity in the picture-elicited narratives of the normal elders.

Although some neurological tests use linguistic aspects such as categories of nouns and syntactic structures to explore possible functions of the brain in experimental psychology or neurology—for example, the Boston Diagnostic Aphasia Examination (BDAE) (Goodglass & Kaplan, 1983) and the Bilingual Aphasia Test (BAT) (Paradis, 1987)—the exploration of the impact of aging through linguistics or from a linguistic perspective is relatively new. The term "Gerontolinguistics" (the study of aging through linguistics, or the interdisciplinary study and collaboration between linguistics and gerontology) was coined by gerontolinguist Makoni in 1997. In Makoni's words, Gerontolinguistics is "a form of disciplined interdisciplinary language" (1997).

However, the problem is that, for a long time, linguistics and its branches (including phonology, lexicology, syntax, and pragmatics) remained rather separate from the aging-related sciences (neurology, psychology, sociology, and education). Linguists, gerontologists, neurologists and psychologists kept their dominant domains strictly under their control for different goals.

The collaboration or integration of linguistics and research in linguistic aspects of aging, such as the elder's language production, would provide a fuller picture of what change can happen in the elder's brain in terms of language production. As Melrose points out, "Much more needs to be done, but it can be best done if the questions neuroscientists ask about language are informed by linguists who have also learned to ask the right questions" (2005, p 419). Thus, the collaboration or integration becomes necessary. A major contribution has been done by Makoni. Makoni has explored aging through discourse analysis (2001), writing history (2000), the structure of narratives (2002) and Dynamic System Theory (2005). His linguistic exploration of aging through Dynamic System Theory (DST) is an important contribution to the study of aging since he has integrated "individual" and "environment" as a whole. DST was originated from mathematics, and has been successfully applied to other sciences such as cognition sciences and language development. "The simplest definition of a dynamic system is: *a system of interaction variables that is constantly changing due to interaction with its environment and self reorganization*" (de Bot and Makoni, 2005, p 5). The main aspects of the DST can be found in the book by de Bot and Makoni (de Bot and Makoni, 2005, p 6).

The success of Makoni in terms of applying Dynamic System Theory to his linguistic exploration of aging sheds light on the study of aging. For example, Makoni, Lin and Schrauf situated their research, the effects of age and education on narrative complexity in older Chinese in the USA, in the framework of DST (de Bot and Makoni, 2005). The results of their study suggest that story telling might be a potentially useful diagnostic tool for older Chinese. However, the Dynamic System Theory was originated from mathematics, and the purpose of its original establishment was not intended for the study of language(s), and thus it might not be able to accurately show how language is used to construe knowledge and the environment. For example, it cannot show how transitivity can be different in the Chinese elders' narratives between different age groups. In order to bridge this gap, the current research will study transitivity in Chinese elders' narratives from the perspective of Systemic Functional Theory (SFT), a well-known linguistic theory that integrates both language and "environment" ([the context]) with a consideration to Chinese language.

Systemic Functional Linguistics (SFT) is a social semiotic theory of language developed by Halliday since the 1970s (1973, 1975, 1978, 1994, and 2004). According to Halliday, language is influenced by context; conversely, context shapes language. Language therefore should be studied and examined in the social environment. Thus, language is a product of context: in Halliday's words "context of situation" (1989, p 46). The key concept in SFT is the "meaning potential of language," which can be realized through three meta-functions: the ideational function, the interpersonal function, and the textual function—in the corresponding register of "field, tenor and mode" (1989, p 12). (A more detailed explanation of SFT will be in Chapter 3)

The integration of language and context in SFT indicates that SFT can provide a fuller picture of language and environment, especially of the actual use of language and the context. Functional linguists such as Fawcett (1980) have taken a more cognitive approach to explore language and social interaction. Halliday himself has moved tentatively toward cognitive direction (Halliday & Matthiessen, 1999, 2000, 2001, 2002). Melrose (2005) has indicated that neurologists can gain insights from the ideational function of SFT, and this function can be used in the study of neurology. Armstrong (2001, 2004) has also applied some SFT principles (ideational, in this case) to the comparative study of Aphasia and normal elders, and she has unveiled some differences between them. The above researches indicate that SFT is a suitable linguistic theory to study aging.

Makoni, Lin and Schrauf have indicated that a theory which has taken Chinese linguistic features into account would be appropriate to the study of Chinese language. They pointed out in their study that "the analysis is complicated because it is difficult to use Western views when analyzing Chinese texts" (Makoni et al. 2005, p117). SFT has taken the Chinese language into account in its development. For example, Chinese philosophy and the way of Chinese thinking have been reflected in the underlying tenets of Halliday's functional linguistic theory.

In all these histories, the wordings and the meaning emerge together. The relationship is that of the two sides of the Stoic-Saussurean sign-- perhaps best represented in the familiar Chinese figure yin and yang (which is in fact just that, a representation of the sign). (Halliday and Matthiessen, 1999, 2000, 2001, 2002, pp 18-19)

Yin refers to the passive, female cosmic principle, and Yang refers to the active, masculine cosmic principle in Chinese dualistic philosophy. The fact that SFT has gained insights from the Chinese language is revealed in the following question and its answer by Halliday:

What is the relation between the code and the culture which creates it, and which it transmits to the next generation? Linguists in the anthropological tradition had tried to establish links with meanings expressed lexically: Eskimo words for 'snow'. Arabic words for 'camel' and so on. Yet vocabulary only 'reflects' culture by courtesy of its internal organization as a whole; and the assertion that 'because "camels" are important to the Arabs, "therefore" they have a lot of different words for "them"' is a statement as much about English as about Arabic. Presumably nothing is more important than rice to the Chinese; yet Chinese has a single word for rice—and it means various other things besides. Chinese happens to be a language of a type that favors general nouns. (Halliday, 2000 p F57)

The above two quotes show that SFT has taken the Chinese language and its views into account and it has reflected the characteristics of the Chinese language; therefore it can be used as a suitable theory to study the Chinese language and aging in the present research.

1.2 Chinese Aging and the Gap in its Research

In terms of Chinese aging, there are basically two problems. One is that there are huge numbers of elderly populations, and aging will thus continue to be a big issue in China. The other problem is that aging is critically under-studied in China.

1.2.1 The Problem of the Elders in China

China has a large population (approximately 1.3 billion at present), which continues to increase. Because of China's size and its birth control policy, Chinese aging population is increasing, both in terms of number and in proportion to the whole population. According to Li, Chi, Zhang and Guo (2006), the population projection shows that more than 243 848 million, or 17.1%, of the total population will reach the age of 60 (usually the age of retirement) by 2020. According to what Ying and Yao published online (September 13, 2006), the number of old people increased to 129 million in 2000, and has since been growing steadily at the rate of 3.2% per year. It is estimated that the number of old people in China will increase to 335 million in the year 2030.

According to Waldman (2005), who quoted a paper published by the

Center for Strategic and International Studies (CSIS) in Washington, D C (Jackson and Howe, 2004), the United Nations (UN) projected that the share of China's population aged 60-and-over will rise to 28 percent by 2040 from 11 percent in 2004, and there will be 397 million Chinese citizens aged 60-plus by 2040 if the current demographic trends continue. This figure is more than the total current populations of France, Germany, Italy, Japan and the United Kingdom combined.

With this huge increase of China's population aged 60-and-over, the Chinese population structure has experienced and will continue to experience a big change. Thirty-eight years ago (1970), Chinese government was concerned that it had too many children to support, and enacted a one-child-per-family policy. The number of children between 0-4 years old was 132 465 thousand in 1970. This number decreased to 96,074 thousand in 2000, and it will further decrease to 71 700 thousand by the year 2050. However, China presently is facing a reverse problem of the one-child policy: China soon will have too few children to support the rapidly-increasing aging population. The number of elders between 60-64 years old increased from 20 980 thousand in 1970 to 41 036 thousand in, and will continue to increase to 104 187 thousand in. Table 1 shows the projected Chinese aging trend in 1970, 2000 and 2050.

Table 1.2.1.1   China Population by Five-Year Age Group and Gender (Thousands)

Age	1970			2000			2050		
	Both genders	Male	Female	Both genders	Male	Female	Both genders	Male	Female
0-4	132 465	68 134	64 331	96 074	51 198	44 877	71 700	37 608	34 092
5-9	109 721	56 618	53 102	103 282	54 510	48 772	71 804	37 822	33 983
10-14	87 853	45 319	42 534	117 418	61 581	55 837	71 895	38 029	33 866
15-19	91 201	46 884	44 318	101 079	52 917	48 162	74 058	39 334	34 724
20-24	67 004	35 237	31 766	96 668	49 789	46 879	79 111	42 179	36 933
25-29	52 582	27 840	24 742	121 268	62 351	58 917	83 789	44 833	38 956
30-34	49 538	26 513	23 025	126 299	65 018	61 281	85 903	45 944	39 958
35-39	48 042	25 525	22 517	104 352	53 712	50 640	85 094	45 496	39 598
40-44	41 588	21 989	19 599	83 192	43 052	40 140	81 672	43 635	38 037

Continued

Age	1970			2000			2050		
	Both genders	Male	Female	Both genders	Male	Female	Both genders	Male	Female
45-49	36 630	19 035	17 594	84 848	43 462	41 385	81 020	43 216	37 805
50-54	31 184	15 876	15 308	61 406	31 826	29 580	89 955	47 395	42 559
55-59	26 082	12 944	13 137	46 302	24 158	22 144	94 990	49 289	45 701
60-64	20 980	9 858	11 122	41 036	21 308	19 728	104 187	53 256	50 931
65-69	15 547	6 864	8 683	34 712	17 565	17 147	83 906	42 159	41 746
70-74	8 911	3 699	5 212	24 870	12 092	12 777	71 596	34 416	37 180
75-79	7 346	3 360	3 986	15 728	7 086	8 643	75 149	34 614	40 535
80-84	2 933	1 246	1 688	7 907	3 207	4 701	57 871	24 973	32 898
85-89	891	345	546	2 740	957	1 783	29 439	11 456	17 984
90-94	157	54	103	677	186	492	11 227	3 808	7 419
95-99	19	5	13	99	21	78	3 884	1 077	2 806
100+	1	0	1	6	1	5	597	139	458

Source: *World Population Prospects: The 2006 Revision* (2007).

This projected huge rapid increase in the aging population in China can cause serious ramifications by the year 2050. This problem can be vividly seen by comparing proportion and size of populations of age 60-and-over between the years of 2000 and 2050 in Figure 1.2.1.1.

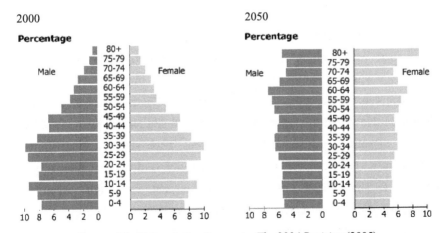

Source: *World Population Prospects: The 2004 Revision* (2005).
Figure 1.2.1.1   Population Pyramids, China: 2000 and 2050

1.2.2 Language-related Chinese Aging Research and its Gap

Chinese aging has been significantly under-studied. Only a few studies can be found on Chinese aging, and they concentrate on physical aspects such as the daily activities and self satisfaction evaluation (Zeng & Vaupel 2002, Woo et al. 1996), and on the neuroepidemiological aspects such as Alzheimer's disease and other dementia disorders in urban communities in Beijing (Wang et al. 2000).

Studies on Chinese aging in relation with language or linguistics are even fewer, and they do not focus much on language and meaning. For example, Noels et al (1999) studied the intergenerational and intragenerational communications between the young and the old in both the United States and China, and they explained the national differences in terms of Communication Accommodation Theory (CAT) (Giles et al. 1992). The significance of CAT is that aging can be explained with regard to the interactions and the environment which elders could/would confront. They studied how the interactions of the young and the old generation influence the elder's speaking style. Although this research is relevant to language, unfortunately language elements (such as form and function of the language) were not fully examined.

Morton et al (1992) compared the role of English in both Chinese and Vietnamese communities. They demonstrated that low English language proficiency was positively correlated with functional impairment in the older Chinese community, but this did not happen in the Vietnamese community in California. However, this might not be true with similar observations in Los Angles. In some small areas in Los Angles. Live almost entire Chinese communities. Nearly every business or activity is done in Chinese from banking to shopping. So my speculation is that low English language proficiency does not influence the Chinese elders there.

A study more related to language has been conducted by Makoni et al (2005). They studied the relationship between age and narrative structures in older Chinese in the USA. Their study did not find a relationship between age and narrative complexity in picture-elicited narratives. While they set a good example for researching Chinese aging from the linguistic perspective, their sample is relatively small and their study is "out of place". (For details, see Chapter 2) The elders lived in New York for a long time and what happened to their language over the years of living in the United States remains unknown. My speculation is that elders in China might perform differently. And my research will fill this gap by examining the elders in China. Also my research will focus more on the linguistic aspects of aging which have not yet fully been studied by the above researchers.

1.3 The Significance of the Present Study

The present study can advance the knowledge of language and aging in Chinese elders, and can provide a new approach to understanding the relationship between language and aging. This study may provide useful information to care-givers and medical professionals; for example, the results of the present study show that there is no obvious language declination among the elderly age groups of 50-79 in the production of picture-elicited narratives. Therefore, if a care-giver or medical professional finds an elder who has an unusual language declination in the production of picture-elicited narratives, and who falls in the age range of 50-79, the care-giver or medical professional can recommend this elder for further diagnosis. It may help a neurologist to understand how an elder patient's brain functions when language is involved; and it may help government policy makers to decide what language facilities they can provide for certain elders.

1.4 Goals of the Present Study

1. To revise and modify the too-generalized results of age impact on language by the previous researchers. [(The previous results: aging

reduces density of informational content (Juncos-Rabadán, Pereiro and Rodríguez, 2005); the ability to understand and tell stories declines with increasing age regardless of language (Juncos-Rabadán, 1996)]

2. To gain a new and detailed understanding of age, education and gender impact on transitivity in Chinese elders, and specifically, to gain the trend of age ability change in the age groups of 50-59, 60-69, and 70-79.

3. To experimentally and statistically test the assumption of Makoni, Lin and Schrauf (2005) that education cannot affect the performance of elders in picture-elicited narratives. The reason for so doing is that certain elements of the picture-elicited narratives can be used as a diagnostic tool if there is no correlation between age and picture-elicited narratives.

4. To explore the insights we can gain about the impact of Chinese aging by using SFT, and to explore how these insights can contribute to an understanding of Chinese aging.

1.5 Brief Descriptions about the Present Research

The present study can fill the gap in Chinese aging from the perspective of SFT. In the present research, the participants were 60 Chinese elders whose age range was from 50-79 years old, and they were equally divided into three age groups of 50-59, 60-69, and 70-79, with 10 males and 10 females in each group. The instrument used to elicit the elderly narratives was the six-panel pictures of "Bird Nest Story" from Paradis BAT (Bilingual Aphasia Test, 1987). The narratives were then encoded by two separate coders according to the coding system. The coding system was developed by the author based on the stimuli of the "Bird Nest Story" (Paradis, 1987) and transitivity in SFT (Systemic Functional Theory) (Halliday, 2000).

The linguistic theory used in the present research is transitivity in SFT. Transitivity is a main system in SFT, and the transitivity system can construe the word of experiences into a manageable set of processes. These processes consist of material process, mental process, verbal process, behavioral process and existential process. The present study analyzes how the participants performed in transitivity as a whole and in each process respectively in terms of age groups.

Although this study examines the age impact on transitivity in Chinese elderly narratives, education and gender can possibly affect the participants' performance on transitivity. Thus GLM (General Linear Model) in ANOVA (Analysis of Variance) was used to analyze the encoded data. In this way not only the factors (age, education and gender) as well as the levels (three age groups, three education level groups and two gender groups) but also the interactions of factors and levels were taken into account.

The results of this study indicate that age can statistically have a significant impact on the participants' performance in transitivity. The points of the participants' performance in transitivity increased from Age Group 50-59 to Age Group 60-69, and the points of participants' performance decreased from Age Group 60-69 to Age Group 70-79. The tendency of the age group's performance in transitivity was like a "∧" shape. Education and gender did not statistically have a significant impact on the overall performance of transitivity between the three age groups (50-59, 60-69 and 70-79).

The conclusions were drawn based on the present study results, and the results supported the hypotheses. After discussing and defending the strengths of the present research, the author critically evaluates the present research by identifying its limitations and suggests directions for future research.

1.6 Chapter Overview

This dissertation is divided into seven chapters. In addition to Chapter 1, the introduction chapter, Chapter 2 reviews the previous literature that relates previous research on the relationship between picture-elicited narratives and aging. It also reviews the previous literature that relates aging and SFT. In addition to a brief description about previous research, the author critically points out both the weaknesses and the strengths of that research. Chapter 3 explains the theoretical framework (SFT) of the present research. This chapter explains how transitivity and each process of transitivity can be used. Chapter 4 describes the information about the participants, the method used to collect the data, and the validity and reliability of data. Chapter 5 explains how the coders are trained and how the data are encoded with examples; it also explains the accuracy of the coders and the inter-reliability of the coders. Chapter 6 gives the results of the present study. Chapter 7 presents the conclusion which incorporates a discussion about the strengths, limitations, and directions for further research and final remarks.

Chapter 2   LITERATURE REVIEW

In this chapter, I give a detailed review of the research done with relation to aging and picture-elicited narratives. I also review the research done with relation to aging under the theoretical framework of transitivity in SFT. Transitivity and SFT will be explained in Chapter 3 in this dissertation. In the end of this chapter, I explain the relation of the present research with the previous research to show the unique role that the present research can play in the continuum of research.

This chapter consists of four sections. In the first section, I will review picture-elicited narratives, which are a major data collection method. This review will include both a brief description of how pictures are used in collecting language production data and comments on the strengths and weaknesses of picture-elicited narratives. In the second section, I will give a detailed review of the research on narratives and aging. It will include four parts: (a) a brief summary of the research, (b) the strengths of the research, (c) the weaknesses of the research, and (d) how the weaknesses can be overcome in the present research. In the third section, I will give a detailed review of the research on aging and/or narratives under the theoretical framework of transitivity. This section also includes four parts with a similar structure as the one in the second section, (a) a brief summary of the research, (b) the strengths of the research, (c) the weaknesses of the research, and (d) how the weaknesses can be overcome in the present research. In the fourth section, I will explain the relation of the present research with the previous research and show its unique role in the field.

2.1 Picture-elicited Narratives

Picture-elicited narrative is a widely used method for collecting language data from children and young adults and has been mainly used in the study of language acquisition and second (foreign) language acquisition (Ratner and Menn, 2000). According to Ratner and Menn, the use and the contribution of pictures in language elicitation can be traced to Berko Gleason (1958). Berko Gleason uses hand-drawn figures of whimsical creatures to elicit language from children (which contains plural forms, past tense, etc.) and studies the child language in terms of language acquisition. Prideaux (1985) comments that Berko Gleason's methodological orientations have proven very valuable and productive, and calls Berko Gleason's work "a landmark in language acquisition research" (Prideaux, 1985 p 9).

Besides Berko Gleason's picture technique being used in language acquisition studies, her picture-story technique has also made a contribution to the study of aphasia. For example, Berko Gleason with her collaborators Goodglass and others develops the Story Completion Test to elicit an attempt each time by any subject (Berko Gleason, Goodglass, Ackerman, Green & Hyde, 1975; Berko Gleason, Goodglass, Obler, Green, Hyde & Weintraub, 1980). And in the test, the elicitation technique with cartoon strips helps the examiners free from the problem of dealing with evasive or off-target responses to a great extent. As a result, Goodglass (2000) praises Berko Gleason's picture elicitation method as a pioneering technique.

Since Berko Gleason (1958), different pictures have been developed and used to elicit narratives from normal adults and adults with aphasia (Rathner and Menn, 2000).

Many scholars have used picture-elicited narratives to study aging and aphasia. For example, the "Cookie Theft" picture is used in Goodglass and Caplan (1983) and Makoni, Lin and Schrauf (2005); and "The Bird Nest Story" is used to elicit narratives in Paradis (1987), Kemper et al., (1990),

Juncos-Rabadan (1994, 1996, 2005), and Makoni, Lin and Schrauf (2005).

Picture-elicited narratives from participants have three strengths. First, the participants have relatively more freedom to use the words and express their ideas about pictures as compared to the strictly controlled psychological laboratory method of pushing a button and completing phrases. Second, picture-elicited narratives allow the researcher to have the knowledge of the content in the pictures and effectively control the content of the language produced. So using picture-elicited narratives increases the predictability and duplicate (or re-test) reliability of the research. Third, picture-elicited narratives allow the narratives to be conveniently elicited outside the strictly controlled psychological experiment laboratories.

However, picture-elicited narratives have their own disadvantages. For example, picture-elicited narratives can be poor in their ecological validity because they may not reflect participants' daily interactions and open-ended spontaneous conversations in a specific situation or culture. Although the participants' daily interactions and open-ended spontaneous conversations could have high ecological validity to show the styles and characteristics of the participants, their low abilities to be duplicated and the researcher's inability to predict and control the content advise against their use in research. This is why present research does not intend to use the participants' daily interactions and open-ended spontaneous conversations.

2.2 Previous Research in Aging Using Picture-elicited Narratives

Research investigating the relationship between narrative structures and aging by using picture-elicited elderly narratives is first made by Kemper and Rash (1990). They find that the syntactic complexity of the narratives declines across age groups. By adopting a scoring system for narrative complexity from earlier work with children by Botvin and Sutton-Smith (1977), they categorize the narrative complexity into eight levels from simple Level 1 to complex Level 8, and they examine the relationship between age and the complexity of the elderly narratives based on the criteria of each level from one to eight. In this way, they construct a measurement for the relation between narrative structures and aging. However, their research has two weaknesses. One weakness of their research is the adoption of a scoring system from research with children. Using a scoring system adapted from work with children assumes that the mechanism responsible for children learning a second or foreign language is quite the same as the mechanism which leads to language decline in the elderly as their age increases. The problem is that these researchers do not approve this assumption. The mechanism responsible for children learning a second or foreign language can be quite different from that responsible for language production in the elderly who have already learned the language. The language resources that children use might be very limited since they are in the process of leaning the language, and their language ability can increase as time goes on (that is, with the increase of age) during learning process. Elderly adults have already grasped the language, the declination of their language production ability can be very slow, and some aspects of language declination remain unknown.

Another weakness of Kemper and Rash (1990) is that the decision of using the complexity of the narrative structure to measure elderly narratives may not work well because the picture-elicited narratives are a kind of language production in which narrators have the freedom to use different language forms. Some may prefer simple narrative structures to complicated narrative structures, and others might do vice versa. For example, "evaluation" or coda is an important criterion for Kemper et al. (1990) and Makoni et al. (2005) to decide the narrative's structural complexity, but in data I collected, I have found that there is no coda or evaluation in some well educated college students' narratives elicited by similar or the same pictures used in the Makoni et al. (2005) study.

Fundamentally, the weakness of Kemper and Rash (1990) is the use of a super structure to measure elderly speakers' narratives, which produced unsatisfactory results. Since the super structure is a kind of form (format), and the format cannot sufficiently generate the meaning, the same kind of bottle can hold different wines. In spite of their weaknesses, one insight from Kemper et al.'s research is that syntactic complexity can be affected in the elderly speakers' narratives.

Juncos-Rabadán (1994) shows the effectiveness of the Bilingual Aphasia Test (BAT) for studying aging and language performance. He investigates the utility of the test for "assessing the effect of age on the capacities of bilingual elderly people at various linguistic levels and skills with a view to determining whether the deterioration affects both languages in the same way" (p 67). Sixty bilinguals in Spanish and Galician are recruited as subjects in the study. The subjects are divided into three age groups with 10 women and 10 men in each group: (1) 30-40 years old, (2) 50-59 years old, and (3) 70-90 years old. The subjects are non-neurological patients at several hospitals in Vigo, Galicia (Galicia is a bilingual region of Spain); all of them agree to participate voluntarily. Educational levels are controlled and they are divided into three groups: low (0-4 years of formal education), middle (5-8 years) and high (9-15 years). Juncos-Rabadán's study confirms that the BAT is a suitable tool for assessing elderly bilinguals, producing results showing that deterioration affects both languages.

This study has three main strengths. First, it establishes a foundation for future studies by pointing out a future research direction: the BAT can be used to study normal aging. Second, while Paradis (1987) explains that the BAT can be used for the study of elderly monolinguals, Juncos-Rabadán's (1994) research takes one step further: BAT data can be used to study normal monolingual elders. Third, Juncos-Rabadán (1994) uses a wide range of ages (from 30 to 90 years old—a span of 60 years), and the age span is extended.

However, this study has five major of weaknesses. First, the age range is not a continuum, namely some age groups are not represented in this research. For example, the group of 60-69 is not represented. Second, the age range is not equally distributed in each group: (1) 30-40 years (M 35.7, SD

3.9), (2) 50-59 year (M 54.8, SD 2.9), and (3) 70-90 year (M 75.9, SD 4.9). The age range is almost 10 years in the first and second groups, while it is 20 years in the third group. Third, the participants are also not evenly distributed. A 10-year span is represented by 20 persons in the first and second groups, while a 20-year span is represented by 20 persons in the third group. Fourth, Juncos-Rabadán does not give an explanation for the age at which the subjects began to use bilingual speech and the motivation for being bilingual, and these factors can affect the results of the research. Fifth, Juncos-Rabadán uses a structural approach to language which separates form and meaning. In my research, the Chinese data are well distributed and matched, overcoming the weakness of the previously mentioned study (see the latter part of my research on the methodology).

Juncos-Rabadán (1996) conducts another cross-linguistic study of elderly participants' capacity to tell stories elicited by a set of pictures. There are 184 subjects grouped by age, gender, years of formal education, and language (Catalan, English, French, Galician, and Spanish). The task requires the subjects to tell the six-picture "The Nest story" from the Bilingual Aphasia Test (BAT) (Paradis, 1987). The results show that the ability to understand and tell stories declines with increasing age regardless of language. Education increases capacity to tell stories, but the sex of the participants has no influence.

Juncos-Rabadán's (1996) research has two main strengths. First, it is a formal study with a large number of participants (184). Second, the participants are from a variety of origins and countries, and they speak different languages, thus the diversity of representation increases as compared with Juncos-Rabadán's (1994) research.

However, this research has seven main weaknesses. First, only two age groups (age 50-59, n=94; and age 70-91, n=90) are selected while the group for age 60-69 is not represented. Second, the age range is not equally distributed: it is 10 years in first group and 20 years in the second group. Third, the participants are also not evenly distributed: 94 participants represent a 10-year span in the first group, while in the second group, 90 participants represent a 20-year span. Fourth, the difference of mean age between the two groups is about 23, a huge difference which may be affected by possible age problems (e.g. the participants can have a declination in health). What could happen in the 23 years remains very unclear. Fifth, education is not evenly distributed across origin (geographical) groups, G and S groups have less education, C, M, and O groups have higher education; Education is also not evenly distributed across age groups, and the age 50-59 group has more education while the age 70-79 group has less education. Sixth, the language terminology used in their publication is rather confusing. For example, sometimes Juncos-Rabadán uses "first language" interchangeably with "native language." Seventh, gender distribution is not mentioned within each group for geographical location and confusion can be caused. All of these weaknesses will be avoided and overcome in my research (see the latter part of data description in the methodology section).

Juncos-Rabadán, Pereiro, and Rodríguez (2005) examine age-related changes in the oral narratives of 79 adults aged 40-91 who told stories from the "The Bird Nest Story" pictures. Again, the six-picture "The Birds Nest story" is used from the Bilingual Aphasia Test (BAT) (Paradis, 1987). They analyze the quantity, information content and cohesion of the narratives using a detailed transcription and codification system. They use a LISREL (Jöreskog and Sörbom, 1993) analysis to study the relationship between narrative performance and age, level of education and verbal capacity. Their results show that aging increases quantity, reduces density of informational content and cohesive reference of narratives and increases the units of irrelevant content.

This research can have three main strengths. First, it is largely based on Juncos-Rabadán (1994, 1996) and in a sense this research is a further development of the previous studies in terms of their study aims and data. Their study aim is more specific: to study the relation between picture-elicited narratives and age and education. Second, the data cover the narratives from continuous age groups. They largely fill the gap of data in previous studies. The age range is a continuum, from age 40 to 91, which fills the missing group of age 60-69 in the previous study. Third, more stimuli are used. One stimulus is "The Bird Nest Story" from the Bilingual Aphasia Test (Paradis, 1987) and the other two ("Walking the dog" and "Burning the dinner") are constructed by the researchers along similar lines specifically for their study. All three stimuli involve everyday events occurring in limited commonplace settings.

However, this study has four main weaknesses. First, the age range is not equally distributed and the age groups are as follows: (1) 40-50 years (M 43.9 SD 2.53), (2) 51-60 years (M 56.25, SD 3.29), (3) 61-70 years (M 65.25, SD 2.56), and (4) 70-91 years (M 75.89, SD 5.44). I speculate that the number in the fourth group may not be correct because the age range was almost 10 years in the first, second, and third groups while the age range was 20 years in the fourth group. Second, the participants are also not evenly distributed. The 10-year age range in the first, second and third groups is represented by 21, 20, and 19 persons respectively, while in the fourth group, a 20-year age range is represented by only 19 persons. Third, the results are limited to the Galician language in the center of Galicia in Northwestern Spain. As Galician language belongs to the Roman language family (which is branch of Indo-European), is derived from Latin, it gives emphasis on structures and forms. Due to different language writing systems and culture, this result cannot extend to Mandarin, which is a Sino-Tibetan language. Fourth, the education between the young groups and the old groups is unbalanced. It may be unfair to conclude that there is a relationship between education and old age because the young groups have more education and the old groups have less education. Due to the limitation of their data, their conclusion may be inaccurate. These kinds of weaknesses will be overcome in my research data (see Chapter 4).

Overall, Juncos-Rabadán gradually switches from research focusing on linguistic structure (see Juncos-Rabadán 1994, 1996) to research focusing on semantics or meaning (see Juncos-Rabadán et al., 2005), as found in the literature above.

To my knowledge, the only study on picture-elicited Chinese narratives is conducted by Makoni, Lin and Schrauf (2005). In their pioneer research, they investigate the role of narratives as a diagnostic tool in Chinese elders in New York City. They focus on storytelling because they thought that "everyone was expected to be able to tell stories irrespective of their level of education, so a 'breakdown' in storytelling could serve as a useful diagnostic tool" (p. 98). According to them, from a Dynamic Systems Theory perspective, storytelling requires the ability to integrate various mental representations (visual, auditory, and haptic). It is the ability to integrate these abilities which they sought to test. They recruited 12 individuals (5 females, 7 males) ranging in age from 63 to 78 (M = 70.25, SD = 5.66), and ranging in years of education from 4 to 18 (M = 12.83, SD = 4.53). All subjects were born in mainland China except for one in New York. The subjects were residing in the senior center on 100 Gold Center, Manhattan, New York City. The elderly subjects were cognitively intact according to their performance on the Short Portable Mental Status Questionnaire (SPMSQ; see Pfeiffer, 1975). Digits forward and backward were also administered to each participant. They used the "Cookie Theft Picture" from the Boston Diagnostic Aphasia examination to elicit stories. In the experiment, the language used in the assessment depended on the informants' preference for Mandarin or Cantonese.

They have found in some cases the subjects code-switched between languages. The coding scheme they used is adopted from Kemper et al. (1990). Their results suggest that storytelling—at least for older Chinese storytellers—might potentially be a useful diagnostic tool because narrative complexity is not necessarily confounded by education.

The contribution of this research is that Makoni, Lin and Schrauf have laid a foundation to show the procedure of how the research on Chinese narratives should be conducted. They have also commented on important literature related to this research and finally they have suggested the cautions that future researchers should consider: "the analysis is complicated because it is not easy to use Western views when analyzing Chinese texts" (p. 117). It is this research that inspired me to conduct the present study.

However, this research has five main weaknesses. First, Makoni et al.'s (2005) research has the same weakness found in Kemper et al.'s (1990) study because Makoni et al. used the narrative structure developed by Kemper et al. which is based on the scoring system meant for analyzing children learning a language. The learning process in first or second language acquisition can be quite different from that used by elderly speakers to produce their native language. The elderly speakers can lose their language very slowly as their age increases if they reach the age range of language declination. Therefore, the critique on Kemper et al. about using the scoring system of children language acquisition also applies to Makoni et al.

Second, the weakness of this research is related to the participants. The sample number of the participants used by Makoni et al. is relatively small: there are 12 elderly participants altogether, which might not be representative of the elderly population. Their participants use different languages, Mandarin and/or Cantonese, and the participants switch the languages from one to another during the narrative elicitation process. It can be that their participants or some of their participants are neither proficient in Mandarin nor in Cantonese, so the problem may be more related to language proficiency than to aging. The subjects are also not evenly distributed according to the gender (their participants consist of 5 females and 7 males).

Third, although Makoni et al. demonstrate that age is correlated with syntactic complexity (a result shared with Kemper et al.), the relation between age and syntactic complexity may not be persuasive. This is because their participants' narratives were elicited by pictures. Since the elderly participants only need to tell a story about the picture, they can make a choice to use words and structures that they like, which is quite different from having to read what has already been written. In fact, some people like to use complicated structures, others like to use simple structures, and sometimes either simple structures or complicated structures may express the same meaning (content).

Fourth, Makoni, Lin, and Schrauf (2005) adopt perspectives which are not appropriate to study Chinese language. This is indicated in Note 2: "the analysis is complicated because it is not easy to use Western views when analyzing Chinese texts" (p.117).

Last, Makoni et al. do not give an explanation as to why Juncos-Rabadán's (1996) research showed that age and education could affect the narratives of the elderly speakers and why Kemper et al. did not find an age and education effect on the elderly speakers' narrative structures.

The weaknesses in Makoni et al. can be avoided in the present research. The present research will use a transitivity analysis based in SFT, and focus both on form and on meaning to study elderly Chinese speakers' narratives. A discussion on the appropriateness for using transitivity to analyze Chinese will be found in Chapter 4. There will be more participants in the present research (see Chapter 4), and the present research will explain why there are contradictions between the previous studies conducted by Kemper et al., Juncos-Rabadán et al. and Makoni et al.

2.3 The Previous Research Using the Insights of Transitivity in SFT

The formal application of SFT to neuroscience, aphasia patients, and normal elderly speakers is quite a recent trend. A few researchers have begun to use the insights of systemic functional linguistics, the transitivity in the ideational function in particular, to study aging and brain function. They have explored aging and brain function by following the six components of transitivity: DOING, SENSING, BEING, SAYING, BEHAVING and EXISTING. A detailed explanation of transitivity will be in Chapter 3.

In the following, I will review research that formally uses the insights from transitivity from SFT. First, Armstrong (2002) conducts some pioneering research in the application of SFT to aphasia research. She argues that SFT can reflect the situation of context. The advantage of using SFT is that both the linguistic form and meaning can be represented, and thus the separation of form and meaning can be avoided. A relative real situation of the participants can be studied.

Armstrong (2002) uses the framework of transitivity in Halliday's SFT to examine the usage and functions of different types of verbs by four aphasic speakers and four normal speakers. She finds that the semantic patterns of verbs used by aphasic speakers are different from those of normal speakers and that the four normal control participants perform better than the four speakers with aphasia when lexical verbs are used for as a measurement.

Armstrong (2005) examines how the aphasia patients' opinions and feelings are expressed linguistically. Armstrong uses transitivity, particularly Halliday's (1994) types of verbs (with an emphasis on mental and relational verbs). The advantage of using SFT is that both the meaning and the form of the linguistic structure of the descriptive speech can be emphasized. Her aim is to examine the ability of aphasic speakers to express opinions, feelings and attitude through the verbs related to mental processes and personal evaluations. Five moderately severe aphasic individuals and five non-brain damaged individuals are recruited in her research. Her participants are divided into two groups with four males and one female in each group. The results show, based on the performance compared with non-brain damaged speakers, that the aphasic individuals have (a) less ability to express opinions, feelings and attitudes by using the verbs related to mental processes and to personal evaluations, (b) less lexical density and (c) more general and high frequency mental verbs. Her research provides insight into the meaning of linguistic structure that individuals use in each of two groups. However, her research does not focus on the impact of age on the meaning of linguistic structure, her samples are relatively small, and gender is not evenly distributed in each group (4 males / 1 female).

Armstrong's (2002, 2005) research has three main strengths. First, her research demonstrates that SFL can be appropriate for examining the linguistic performance of aphasia patients and normal elderly speakers, and that SFL can be used in the study of comparative linguistic performance between these two speaker groups. Second, she shows that the advantage of using SFL is that both the linguistic form and meaning can be integrated in the processes (of the transitivity) in language production at the same time. Third, she demonstrates how SFL can be used in the actual research, especially the use of transitivity (material, mental, verbal, relational, existential and behavioral processes) in her research.

However, Armstrong's research has three weaknesses. First, Armstrong uses SFT in her studies, but she does not discuss or make a critique of the weakness of SFT. Second, Armstrong's samples are relatively small: in the 2002 study, there are four normal controls and four aphasia speakers; and in the 2005 study there are five speakers with mildly to moderately severe aphasia and five non-brain damaged speakers matched for age, gender, and years of education. Third, there are no fine-tuned studies of only the patents or elderly speakers. This is because it is expected that it is more difficult to find intra-speaker differences than inter-speaker differences.

The present research will overcome the weaknesses of Armstrong's studies in the following ways. First, the present study will not only use SFL as a guiding linguistic theory, but also will discuss and criticize the weakness of SFL in the research. Second, the present research will use a larger number of participants (60) than those used in Armstrong's research. Third, the present research will be fine-tuned by studying intra-speaker language performance of normal elderly speakers.

Melrose (2005) argues that insights from SFT can be useful to explore key concepts in neuroscience, such as the mirror neuron system, the role of the frontal lobes, and the distributed nature of noun and verb processing. Melrose demonstrates that basic principles of systemic functional linguistics are supported by research in neuroscience, and can point the way forward to future research. SFL can "be able to tell neuroscience something meaningful about language that could lead to even more revealing research" (p. 418).

The strength of this research is that Melrose shows that some basic principles of systemic functional linguistics (for example, the six processes of transitivity) are supported by research in neuroscience by using data and research from others. Melrose shows a relation between transitivity and neuroscience, and calls for cooperation between neuroscientists and linguists. However, the weakness is that Melrose does not point out how neuroscientists and linguists can cooperate, and Melrose does not conduct practical research in this field. The present research will analyze the Chinese narratives in terms of transitivity which, according to Melrose, is supported by neuroscience.

2.4 The Relation of the Present Research with the Previous Research

Despite differences between the studies of Makoni, Armstrong and the present research, these studies are in a complimentary relationship. For example, the transitivity analysis used in the present research could be extended to Makoni's (2002) data. As shown in the dialogue, the use of transitivity can explain the purpose of the nurse and the relationship between the nurse and the elderly speaker.

　(1)　Nurse/Patient Dialogue (from Makoni, 2002, p 815)

　　　Nurse 1: move up (pause) please darling

　　　Resident: I don't want

　　　Nurse 2: carry on

　　　Nurse1: you must mo!

　　　Nurse 2: move up move up (pause) your pillows

　　　Nurse 1: move up Mrs. Smith you must eat now

　　　Nurse 2: move up be a darling

The verb use in the dialogue is summarized in Table 2.4.1. As seen from the table, it can be found that more material verbs were used than the "mental verb 'want'". This indicates that the resident may have fewer reactions to the two nurses and that the resident may have less freedom there. On the one hand, this linguistic analysis might strengthen Makoni's argument about "the controlling dimension of discourse" in terms of power relations in his South Africa. On the other hand, Makoni's research could provide a direction to the present research in terms of how to differentiate the ideology from the linguistic aspects.

Table 2.4.1   Extension to Transitivity

Verbs	Transitivity	Total Numbers
Move (mo)	Material	5
Carry	Material	1
Want	Mental	1
Total		7

The present research can be considered to be an extension to the research of Makoni, Lin and Schrauf (2005). The present research has largely increased the number of participants in Makoni, Lin and Schrauf. Compared with 12 participants in the research of Makoni, Lin and Schrauf, the present research has 60 participants. The present research also finds a solution to theoretical problem raised in Makoni, Lin and Schrauf (2005) (see Chapter 3).

Armstrong's research is very pathologically oriented. For example, she uses transitivity in SFL to compare the linguistic performance of the aphasia patients and the normal elderly speakers. Her strength is that she is from the profession of a speech pathology and she has more experience with the aphasia patients. The weakness of her research is that she mainly applies SFT to her research (2002, 2005), and does not critique the weakness of SFT and then apply SFL in a creative way. However, Armstrong's research can throw light on the present research, and the present research will expand the research done by Armstrong through studying 60 normal elderly participants.

The present research will use more participants than Armstrong's research, and more nuanced intra-group differences may be reflected in the normal elderly group. The present research will critique SFT, show the weakness of SFT, and show how SFT can be used in a creative way. Finally, the critical use of SFL can possibly expand Armstrong's research vision.

Although the present research has a complimentary relation with previous research, it has its uniqueness in the area that it explores. A clear and brief distinction of the present research from the previous is made in Table 2.4.2.

Table 2.4.2   A Comparison of the Present Research with Previous Research

Names / Features	Giles	Makoni	Armstrong	Present Research
Theory	Communication Accommodation	Language Ideology, CDA, DST, Sometimes structural approach to examining social problems (verbal fluency, category fluency, narrative structures	SFL (without critics) Social and Functional	SFL (with critics) Social and Functional
Language	Bilingual	Monolingual, bilingual and multilingual	Monolingual (English)	Monolingual (Chinese)
Goal	Intergenerational, young groups, old groups	Conversations or language related to aging, caregivers, etc. in African and African-American Communities	Mainly aphasia patients, patients with stroke, the comparison between aphasia patients and normal elderly speakers	Mainly normal elderly Chinese

Continued

Names ╲ Features	Giles	Makoni	Armstrong	Present Research
Linguistic aspects	The style of talk	Power, race, communication dialogue, lexical items, narrative structures	Ideational, interpersonal, Textual	Mainly ideational, but also interpersonal and textual
Focus	Inter-generational relation	Power relation	The relation between linguistics and aphasia patients	The relation between linguistics and normal elderly speakers
Gradience	More social aspects	Social and linguistic	Study and compare inter-aphasia patients and normal elderly speakers from social linguistic perspective	More refined study and compare intra-normal elderly speakers and patients from social linguistic perspective
Place	Out of place (immigrants) The United States	In place and out of place (non-immigrants and immigrants) South Africa and the United States	In place Australia	In place China

In conclusion, the present research is different from the previous research in the way that it is a more fine-tuned study focusing on the impact of age on linguistic performance of the elderly Mandarin native speakers in China. It can play a unique role in the continuum of the related research.

Chapter 3   THEORETICAL FRAMEWORK

Chapter 2 reviewed the literature related to the present research. Chapter 3 explains the theoretical framework for transitivity used in the present research. Transitivity is a core component of SFT developed by Halliday in the 1960s and continuously modified by him till present. This chapter also explores the compatibility of transitivity and Chinese (see page 52). In order to explain transitivity and its role in SFT, a brief introduction to SFT is necessary. Therefore, this chapter consists of four sections: a brief introduction to SFT, transitivity in SFT, transitivity applied to health and neuroscience, and transitivity related to Chinese language.

3.1 A Brief Introduction to SFT

As briefly mentioned in Chapter 1, the present research uses SFT as a theoretical framework to study Chinese narratives. Today several leading scholars have researched in the field of SFT worldwide, such as Halliday (2004) and Martin (1992) in Australia, Berry (1996) and Fawcett (1987) in UK, Gregory (1967) in Canada, and Hu (2005) and Huang (1996) in China. Among the above scholars, Halliday's work in SFT is the most influential. Therefore, the present research uses Hallday's SFT as a theoretical framework.

The following section begins with a brief introduction to Halliday's systemic functional theory. Then it explains the difference between Halliday, Martin and Berry. Finally it discusses overlap of Halliday's SFT with other theories such as Vygotsky's social cultural theory and Berstein social theory.

3.1.1 A Brief Introduction to Halliday's SFT

SFT is a social semiotic theory of language developed by Halliday since the1960s (1966, 1967, 1968, 1973, 1975, 1978, 1985, 1994, 2000 and 2004). Halliday's conceptualization of language is typically described as originating with Western thinkers, most notably the British anthropologist Malinowski and his colleague Firth, but his conceptualization of language is also influenced by Chinese language and linguistic theory. Examples of Chinese ideology in Halliday's theory appear in Chapter 1 and also in the section on transitivity in this chapter.

Halliday treats language as foundational for the construction of social experience. For Halliday, language cannot be dissociated from meaning, which has its basis in a complex relationship between function and "context of situation". A key concept in Halliday's approach is the "context of situation" which emerges "through a systematic relationship between the social environment on the one hand, and the functional organization of language on the other" (Halliday, 1985, p11). According to Halliday, the three main metafunctions of language are: ideational, interpersonal, and textual; and field, tenor, and mode are the three central principles necessary for analyzing context. The following section first explains the three metafunctions, and then explains the three principles for contextual analysis.

A general view about components of SFT is shown in Figure 3.1.1:

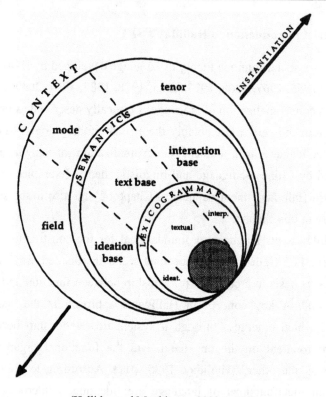

(Halliday and Matthiessen 2002, p 383)

Figure 3.1.1　Stratal and Metafunctional "address" in the Overall Resources

According to Halliday and Hasan (1989), language has three metafunctions: **Ideational, Interpersonal, and Textual.**

1. **Ideational:** The ideational function explains the content, experience, everyday logic, etc. It consists of the following topics: Transitivity: (1) material process, (2) mental process, (3) relational process, (4) behavioral process, (5) verbal process and (6) existential process; and Voice: (1) middle and (2) non-middle (active and passive voice). An explanation of the details of the processes of transitivity appears in the transitivity section, later in this chapter. As an explanation of voice, middle voice signals involvement of only one participant in a sentence. An example of middle voice is "The glass broke."

Non-middle voice signals two or more participants' involvement in a sentence. For example: three participants are involved in "She gives me this book." (active voice), and two participants are involved in "The glass was broken by the cat." (passive voice).

2. **Interpersonal:** Interpersonal function explains the social circumstances of speech, the role of the participants, the power relationship and cultural issues of the participants.

3. **Textual:** The textual function shows the ways in which language organizes itself. It consists of the following components: 1) theme and rheme, 2) information unit: given and new, 3) cohesion: reference, ellipsis, substitution, lexical conjunction, etc.

The three metafunctions can be integrated in Table 3.1.1:

Table 3.1.1   Metafunctional Integration in the Structure of the Clause

	One summer evening	*the Rabbit*	*saw*	*two strange beings creep out of the bracken*
textual	Theme	Rheme		
interpersonal	Adjunct	Subject	Finite/Predicator	Complement
	Resi-	Mood	-due	
ideational	Time	Senser	Process	Phenomenon
	nom. gp.	nom. gp.	verbal gp.	clause: nonfinite

(From Halliday and Matthiessen 2002, p 11)

According to Halliday and Hasan (1989), the three principles used for context analysis are **Field, Tenor, and Mode.**

The analysis of context can be broken down into field, tenor and mode, and for the sake of conciseness, an extended extract from Halliday explains the meanings of field, tenor and mode:

1. **Field** refers to what is happening, to the nature of the social interaction that is taking place: what is it that the participants are engaged in, in which the language figures as some essential component?

2. **Tenor** refers to who is taking part, to the nature of the participants, their status and roles: what kinds of role relationship obtain among the participants, including permanent and temporary relationships of one kind or another, both the types of speech role that they are taking on in the dialogue and the whole cluster of socially significant relationships in which they are involved?

3. **Mode** refers to what part the language is playing, what is that the participants are expecting the language to do for them in that situation: the symbolic organization of the text, the status that it has, and its function in the context, including the channel (is it spoken or written or some combination of the two?) and also the rhetorical mode, what being achieved by the text in terms of such categories as persuasive, expository, didactic and the like.

(Halliday and Hasan 1989, p. 12)

To summarize, field answers the question of what is happening; tenor answers the question of who is taking part; and mode answers the question of what part of language is playing.

3.1.2 The Difference between Halliday and Martin

Notably, other scholars have different ideas on linguistic models and have made different contributions to SFT. For example, Martin (1992) managed to build his own context model for the purpose of education. In so doing, Martin tried to find a midway between Gregory and Halliday. Gregory (1967) thought the "context of situation" consist of four aspects: field, mode, personal and functional tenor, which is different from Halliday's division of "context of situation" which has three aspects: field, mode, and tenor. In order to avoid the confusion between Gregory's functional tenor and Halliday's tenor, Martin used the term "genre" to rename Gregory's functional tenor (Martin and Rothery, 1986). According to Martin, "genre" refers to the language used to represent a staged, goal oriented, social process. Martin also used "register" to replace Halliday's "context of situation," which covered field, mode and tenor.

In addition to his contribution in genre, Martin asserted a higher and more abstract layer above genre, and this layer is ideology. Ideology can form a cultural coded tendency system which can cause language users to choose genre, register and language according to their social classes, genders, ages and races. Ideology is the highest layer in Martin's model, as depicted in the following figure.

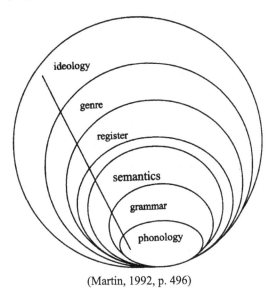

(Martin, 1992, p. 496)

Figure 3.1.2 Martin's SFT Model

The above figure demonstrates that Martin's SFT model is different from Halliday's model (see page 36). Martin divided Halliday's "context of situation" into register, genre and ideology. Martin's register covered Halliday's concepts about register and "context of situation." Halliday defined register as "the configuration of semantic resources that the member of the culture associates with a situation type. It is the meaning potential that is accessible in a given social context" (Halliday, 1978, p. 111). But Martin did not give a clear definition for register. Martin defined genre as a staged, goal oriented social process. For Martin, genre is a connotative semiotic and its expressive form is register. For Halliday, genre is an aspect of mode—although he also notes that a genre "may have implications for other components of meaning" (Halliday, 1978, p. 145), it is included in the notion of register.

As far as ideology is concerned, difference also exists between Martin and Halliday. Martin argues that ideology is a separate higher level. Accordingly, this level is required because "meaning potential" is not evenly distributed across a culture. Ideology is expressed through the content form of genre, register and language. Interestingly, Martin has recently abandoned ideology as a separate level; now, he argues for a new approach to studying ideology which consists of logogenesis, ontogenesis, and phylogenesis. Logogenesis explains how subjects engage dynamically with texts; ontogenesis explains the development of social subjectivity, and phylogenesis explains the ways in which a culture reworks hegemony across generations. Halliday does not frequently use the term "ideology", but he does use an equivalent term, Bernstein's "code" or "sociolinguistic coding orientation," the "particular sub-cultural angle on the social system" that controls the semantic styles of the culture (Halliday, 1978, p 111, 123).

Ultimately, the difference between Halliday and Martin remains in the aspect of "context of situation" in SFT, and this belongs to the ideological aspect of SFT. Their difference does not lie in the ideational function in SFT, so their difference will not influence the use of transitivity in the present research and thus, not particularly relevant to the present research.

3.1.3 The Difference between Berry and Halliday

Berry, specialized in the field of textlinguistics, grammar and context, attended more to the application of text linguistics. In the UK particularly, SFT has metamorphosed into language and ideology and English for specific purposes, and Berry is a good example in this direction. She applied Halliday's SFT to teaching English for specific purposes, particularly, teaching written English for specific purposes. The application work in which she has engaged, together with other colleagues in Nottingham, is a description of the written language of business and industry intended to assist teachers in British schools and universities to prepare students for work in business and industry. The teachers are the intended users of Berry and her colleagues' description of the written language for business and industry. In the description, Berry and her colleagues communicated with teachers, other non-linguists and professionals in non-academic fields for responses and information. The received input allowed Berry and her colleagues to describe the theme, the genre, etc. of the written English in business and industrial contexts and to show how success can be achieved through analyzing themes. Berry and her colleagues concentrate their efforts on describing written discourses which have meaning for teachers, and for professionals in business and industry. Their description can greatly contribute to teaching English for specific purposes.

The theory behind the description of written English for a specific purpose by Berry and her colleagues is Halliday's SFT. As early as 1964, Halliday, McIntosh and Strevens argued for producing text books and other teaching materials for specific purposes such as English for medicine, law, police, business, etc. In a sense, Berry and her colleagues' descriptive project is the application of SFT. Berry argues that one of the great strengths of Halliday's work is its applicability to text analysis, and she acknowledged a debt to Halliday: "In the course of my discussion of a text linguistic perspective, I hope to show something of the enormous debt that I, like so many other text linguists, owe to Halliday and to his innovatory approach the text analysis" (Berry, 1996, p 3)

Berry argues that Halliday's systemic functional approach is ideally suitable for meeting the needs of her research in the description of written English for specific purposes. According to Berry, this is because SFT's design is applicable to texts: it comes complete with a theory of text –context relations; it gives priority to meaning, and it provides a theory of language use as choice. However, Berry's research is limited to written text and context in education; particularly, Berry is limited to themes, themes' determination, etc. She does not make contributions to Halliday's transitivity, which the present research will apply in the analysis in Chapter 5.

3.1.4 The Overlap between Halliday, Vygotsky and Bernstein

Notably, SFT has some overlap with other powerful analytical approaches such as those used by Vygotsky and Bernstein although no clear evidence exists showing who influenced whom. The reason for the overlap can be a sharing of the same or similar objects and context in studying language. For example, Halliday studies meaning and meaning potential in the context; Vygotsky studies signs as mediations, and for Vygotsky, the signs are culturally determined and have meaning. So the overlap between Halliday and Vygotsky are the meanings and the signs. They both attempt to explain the role of language in cultural as well as individual development. Halliday systematically studies the meaning systems of signs, and the results of Halliday's research can facilitate Vygotsky scholars to use signs as mediation. In a sense, Halliday's theory is compatible to Vygotsky's theory. A detailed explanation for the compatibility between theories of Halliday and Vygotsky can be found in Wells (1999).

Overlap also exists between Halliday and Bernstein. Bernstein has made a remarkable contribution to the research of understanding class as culture. He has discovered that class differences in speech were profound enough to demonstrate that language is actually used for different purposes. He has found that these differences are reflected in two different linguistic "codes": the "elaborated code" and "restricted code." The "elaborated code" is used in the middle class group, and the "restricted code" is used in the working class group (Bernstein, 1971, 1990). The participants of different class groups (the middle class group and working class group) in Bernstein's research overlaps with Halliday's tenor, Halliday's tenor explains the nature of the social status of the participants. The language difference in Bernstein's research overlaps with Halliday's mode; in this case, Halliday's mode explains the language used self-consciously by the participants.

In a sense, Bernsteins research enriches Halliday's SFT to some extent. Apparently Bernstein studies the language difference caused by class: middle class group and working class group, but the underlying cause of the differences in language can be educational and financial status of the participants or the participants' families, which is not investigated by SFT.

Despite the overlaps existing between Halliday, Vygotsky and Bernstein, they have different focuses on their research. Halliday focused on language meaning in the context; Vygotsky focused on using signs as mediation, and Bernstein focused on class language. The relationship between Halliday, Vygotsky and Bernstein is complementary, rather than substitutive. Each of them has his own contributions. Hasan (2005) summarizes their contribution as follows:

> Vygotsky contributes to the understanding of our mental life by revealing its deep connection to semiosis; in so doing, he anticipates the literature on the dialectic of language and mind: it is this dialectic that is responsible for their co-evolution in the human species.

> Halliday contributes to the understanding of our semiotic life by revealing its deep connection with society; in so doing, he elaborates on the dialectic of language and society which underlies their co-genesis.

> Bernstein contributes to the understanding of our social life in modern societies by revealing its inherent connection with consciousness created in semiosis in the contexts of communal living; in so doing, he makes us realise how minds need societies and societies need semiosis to survive, to develop, and to change.

(Hasan, 2005, p. 156)

Since the overlaps between Halliday, Vygotsky and Bernstein will not theoretically affect Halliday's transitivity in the present research, further comment is unnecessary.

3.2 Transitivity

As mentioned at the beginning of this chapter, the theoretical framework used to analyze Chinese narratives in the present research is transitivity. Transitivity is a backbone for the ideational function in Halliday's SFT which was briefly explained earlier, and transitivity has been used as a powerful analytic approach. The subsequent discussion is a detailed explanation of transitivity, and includes the position of transitivity in SFT, the development of transitivity in SFT, the content of transitivity, the difference between transitivity and the traditional transitive verbs versus intransitive verbs, and transitivity—an intersection of SFT and other linguistic schools.

3.2.1 The Position of Transitivity in SFT

Transitivity is a key notion in SFT; it refers to how meaning is represented in a language. Transitivity can be a powerful analytic approach to ideation or representation of experience. It can show how speakers encode their mental picture of reality in language, and how they account for their experience of the world around them. Since transitivity's concern is the transmission of ideas, it falls within the realm of the ideational function, one of the three metafunctions in SFT. The other two metafunctions are interpersonal and textual, which have been introduced in the previous part of this chapter.

3.2.2 The Development of Transitivity

Halliday researched, theorized and continued to update transitivity (system) for over forty years. In order to make the transitivity system more complete and practical to construe experience, Halliday has been revising it since the 1960s. Halliday (1966) defined transitivity as the name given to a network of systems whose point of origin is the "major" clause, the clause containing a predication. He further explained that "the transitivity systems are concerned with the type of process expressed in the clause, with the participants in this process, animate and in animate, and with various attributes and circumstances of the process and the participants" (Halliday, 1966, p 38).

Halliday (1985) revised the notion of transitivity in his functional grammar. Transitivity refers to semantic systems of the language, and its function is to sort the "goings-on" into processes, the "goings-on" consist of doing, happening, feeling and being in a language. And the "most powerful conception of the reality" is constituted in the "goings-on" (Halliday, 1985, p 101). Transitivity can also specify clause structures. For example, a clause may include a process, participant(s), and circumstance(s). In my opinion, transitivity is more related to the semantic meaning and grammatical structures.

Halliday (1994) further revised his concept of transitivity in the second edition of his functional grammar. Halliday added elements to the "goings-on" that appeared in the first edition in 1985, and the new "goings-on" consist of happening, doing, sensing, meaning, being and becoming. He changed the "most powerful conception of reality" into the "most powerful impression of experience" (Halliday, 1994, p 106). Thus the "most powerful impression of experience" became a constituent in the "goings-on". He put all these "goings-on" in the grammar of clause, and he clearly indicated that the grammatical system achieved by this is transitivity. The transitivity system can construe world experience into a manageable set of process types.

Halldiay and Matthiessen (2004) revised Halliday's previous concept of transitivity by re-explaining "goings-on". According to them, the "goings-on" or a flow of events is chunked into quanta of change by the grammar of clause: each quantum of change is modeled as a figure—a figure of happening, doing, sensing, being or having (see Halliday and Matthiessen, 1999) (Halldiay and Matthiessen, 2004, p 170). All figures consist of a process unfolding through time and of participants directly involved in the process to some extent. Circumstances of time, space, cause, etc. may exist. These circumstances are attendant on the process, and they are not directly involved in the process. Halldiay and Matthiessen repeat that the grammatical system achieved by this is transitivity, and the transitivity system can construe the world experience into a manageable set of process types. But they further explain that each process type can provide its own model or schema for construing a particular domain of experience.

3.2.3 The Content of Transitivity

Halliday's transitivity contains six processes: material, relational, mental, verbal, behavioral and existential (Halliday, 1985, 1994, 2004). The definition of each process can be found in the comparison of transitivity with the traditional verbs in Table 3.2.4.1. The following examples of each process are from Melrose (2005, p 404):

1. His appearance—it really hit me right between the eyes (DOING, Material).

2. I saw this really sick-looking person (SENSING, Mental).

3. He was so pale and sick-looking (BEING, Relational).

4. His appearance spoke volumes (SAYING, Verbal).

5. He whinged all the time about his health (BEHAVING, Behavioral).

6. There was something really terrible about his appearance (EXISTING, Existential).

The processes are used as the backbone of the ideational function to construe experience of the world. Halliday's transitivity can explain the potential meanings and the realization of meanings. In this sense, Halliday's transitivity is an integration of both meaning and form.

3.2.4 The Difference between Halliday's Transitivity and the Traditional Transitivity

A necessary observation is that Halliday's transitivity is different from traditional transitivity. Traditionally transitivity is divided into transitive and intransitive verbs in terms of syntax. The syntactic distinction between transitive and intransitive verbs depends on whether or not the verbs can take an object. The problem of this syntactic distinction oversimplifies or neglects some important differences of meaning between various types of verbs and the processes the verbs designate. The distinctions of meaning behind transitivity are more than the simple distinction expressed by transitive verbs versus intransitive verbs. A main insight of Halliday's transitivity is that transitivity is the foundation of representation, and provides a path for using transitivity to analyze events and experiences. The following table is an explanation of some aspects of transitivity in comparison with the traditional analysis:

Table 3.2.4.1   Transitivity in Comparison with the Traditional Verb Functions

Transitivity	Definition	Functions	Examples	Traditional Verb Functions
Material	Processes of "doing"	Recounting actions, events, happenings	break, walk, cancel	Transitive; Intransitive
Relational	Processes of "being", and "having"	Description, evaluation/opinion, categorization, connections of discourse participants	He had a car. He is a student. He has a Toyota.	Transitive; Intransitive
Mental	Processes of sensing: feeling, thinking, and perceiving	Perception, reaction, cognition	see, believe, know, like	Transitive; Intransitive
Verbal	Processes of "saying"	Reporting conversation, metaphorical usage	say, talk, praise, tell	Transitive; Intransitive
Behavioral	Physiological/ Psychological processes	Reporting of physiological and psychological "actions"	smile, cough, dream	Transitive; Intransitive
Existential	Processes of existing	Expressing existence	be, exist	Intransitive

3.2.5 Transitivity—the Intersection of SFT and Other Schools of Linguistics

Verbs, the main concern of transitivity, are such important elements (category/function) in grammar that they have long been given great attention. They have been studied by different linguistic schools as common objects. For example, the traditional perspective such as that of Jesperson (1965), Quirk, et al. (1985) studied verbs in terms of category and syntactic functions with some explanation of the semantic meanings. The structural perspective, such as that of Bloomfield (1933) and Chomsky (1957) (from the origin of Bloomfield) studied verbs and described verbs in terms of Immediate Constituents and Transformational Rules. Halliday and Matthiessen (2004) studied verbs from the social and functional perspective, and they described the verbs in terms of ideational, interpersonal and textual metafunctions. In a sense, verbs form an intersection of different schools of linguists although they have different focuses. Both the traditional linguists and the structural linguists study verbs in terms of form and structure; in contrast, systemic functional linguists study verbs by the integration of form and meaning, which is the direction of the present research.

3.2.6 Transitivity in Neurological and Health Science Research

Transitivity has been supported by experimental studies in neurology, and a possible link exists between meaning of verbs and localization in human brain. Thus, the meaning of verbs can possibly become a window in studying the functions of human brain. Detailed evidence can be found in Melrose (2005) who explained how systemic functional linguistics can shed light on the neurological account of language (see literature review in Chapter 2).

Practically, a few pilot studies using the processes of transitivity to examine the function of the elders' brain have proved both feasible and meaningful. Insights gained by the researchers could not possibly be obtained otherwise. For example, Armstrong (2001) found the difference between the lexical verbs and their meanings used by the participants of her study. In 2005 she studied the use of mental meaning of aphasia speakers and found that they used fewer verbs to express mental process. As Armstrong indicated, the study of transitivity is the direction for the future research (For more details about Armstrong's research, see literature review in Chapter 2).

3.3 Chinese and Transitivity

3.3.1 The Compatibility of Transitivity for Studying Chinese

The development of transitivity studies has been influenced by studies on Chinese, and it is compatible with Chinese. As mentioned in the introduction chapter, SFT explores the meaning in context, and it can be an appropriate linguistic theory to study Chinese narratives. Halliday (1999, 2000, 2001, 2002) not only explained the relationship of the words and the meaning—the two sides of the Stoic-Saussurean sign—in terms of Chinese Yin and Yang (representing Chinese ideology) (see Chapter 1), but also used the Chinese ideology of Yin and Yang to explain the semantic system of transitivity. The Chinese Yin and Yang can be clearly found in the following figure although he did not mention Yin and Yang.

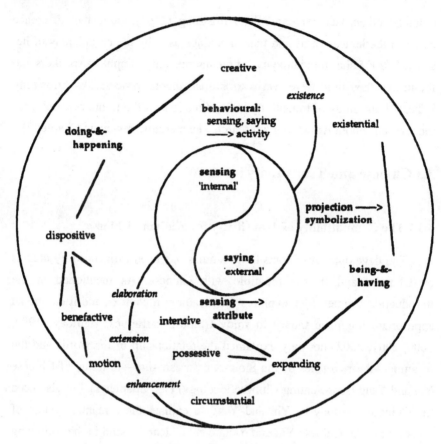

(Halliday and Matthiessen, 1999 p 137)

Figure 3.3.1.1   The Ideas of Yin and Yang in Transitivity

The Chinese Yin and Yang represent an aspect of Chinese philosophy which can account for how the Chinese understand the universe, reality, change and exchange. More details about Yin and Yang can be found in the ancient Chinese book—*Book of Changes* completed in the twelfth century B. C. The figure of Yin and Yang (see below) is usually represented in the shape of arches in a circle (with extensions).

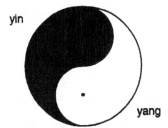

Figure 3.3.1.2   The Figure of Chinese Yin and Yang

Obviously the concept of Figure 3.3.1.2 appeared in Figure 3.3.1.1 to some extent. And the conception of change in Yin and Yang has also been introduced in transitivity. For example, in Halliday and Matthessen's words, "each quantum of change is modeled as a figure—a figure of happening, doing, sensing, being or having" (Halldiay and Matthiessen 2004, p 170). In this case, Figure 3.3.1.1 is viewed as change, and thus, it becomes dynamic, and it can represent a flow of events.

Therefore, ideologically, transitivity is compatible with an aspect of Chinese philosophy. And a theoretical solution is found to solve the problem raised by Makoni, Lin and Shchrauf (2005) as "the analysis is complicated because it is difficult to use Western views when analyzing Chinese texts" (Makoni et al., 2005, p117), namely, transitivity can be a powerful analytic approach to Chinese narratives.

3.3.2 Chinese Scholars' Research in Transitivity

Chinese scholars have gained fruitful results in the research of SFT and the application of SFT to Chinese. Their research has explored whether or not transitivity in SFT can be applied to Chinese language study. For example, Hu, Zhu and Zhang (1989) and Hu, Zhu, Zhang and Li (2005) compare the use of SFT in English and Chinese, and conclude the systemic functional linguistics can be generally applied to Chinese with a few exceptions. This section focuses on the transitivity studies, which will be used in the present research.

Zhou (1999) explores the transitivity system in material clauses in Mandarin Chinese from the perspective of systemic functional linguistics. The strength of this research is that it provides a new description of the semantic choices and syntactic structure in material clauses and classifies the type and subtype of transitivity in terms of the number of participants. The weakness of Zhou's study is that though the number of participants can only provide some general idea of the material process, it does not study other aspects of material process in terms of sub-meaning, which is be due to the complicated Chinese transitivity system.

Cheng (2002) studies relational process in transitivity and suggests that the relational processes are the most difficult to conceptualize and subcategorize. The strength of this research is that it raises the question; the weakness is that it does not find satisfactory answer.

Pan (2003) studies how the transitivity analysis is applied to analyze descriptions in different genres and found more mental processes are used in journals than in advertising. And Pang also find that more material processes and relational processes are found in advertising than that in journals. The strength is Pan applied transitivity to actual analysis; the weakness is that Pan's samples (only one journal and one advertisement) are too small, and generalization may not be extended to other instances.

Ding (2007) comprehensively explores the three semantic levels in the ideational metafunction and find that the semantic scale shows the degree of complexity related to the composition of semantic units. The weakness of this study is that it is not applied to Chinese.

In conclusion, transitivity is compatible with Chinese, and Chinese scholars' research in transitivity and/or in the application of transitivity have/has contributed to understanding and further application of transitivity. Arguably, a detailed and critical study of transitivity can also expand the vision of some relevant researchers in understanding how language functions in neurological and health science.

Chapter 4   METHODOLOGY

The previous chapter explained the theoretical framework used in the present research. This chapter provides the hypotheses which are based on the literature review and theoretical framework. Also explained is the methodology employed to explore the hypotheses. The methodology includes data collection, structure of the data, purpose of using the data as wells as adjustment made for the present coding system in order to render the content more valid than Paradis' (1987) stimuli.

4.1 Hypotheses

Based on the previous research reviewed in Chapter 2 and the theoretical framework of transitivity in SFT described in Chapter 3, the following hypotheses are formulated:

1. Transitivity, a core concept in SFT, is a proper method to study aging and reveals more aspects of aging, especially aging with regard to the characteristics of Chinese language.
2. No obvious, significant age and education impact exists for the use of transitivity in Chinese elders' picture-elicited narratives.
3. A relationship exists between age and the transitivity of the narrative, but this relationship can be contrary to the traditional notion of declination in content as one ages.
4. The relationship between age and transitivity is not a straight linear one. For example, content can increase as age increases to a certain extent; when a certain age is reached, the content can decrease with the increase of age.

5. The analysis of elders' narratives sheds light on transitivity and allow the expansion of transitivity.

4.2 Data Collection

The data used in the present research to test the hypotheses are secondary analysis from Chinese BAT (Bilingual Aphasia Test) Norm, which was a part of the BAT Normative Study directed by Paradis from the 1980s to the 1990s. The purpose of the BAT Normative Study was to obtain BAT Norms from numerous languages spoken by native speakers whose ages were between 50 and 79 years old. In the BAT Normative Study, the norms were obtained from 60 non-brain damaged and non-psychotic subjects in each language in the country where the native languages for the test were spoken.

BAT was designed to be a diagnostic test for hospital patients. When a patient's native language is unavailable or unknown to the hospital staff, the patient can be asked to choose a familiar language from the BAT, and thus, the diagnostic test can be given. The result of the patient's test in the unknown language (Chinese, in this case) is comparable to the result in the language that the hospital staff knows. According to Paradis, BAT can be used quite reliably as a screening instrument (Paradis, 1987, p 19).

BAT examines language performance in four modalities: hearing, speaking, reading and writing. According to Paradis (1987), language performance in each modality is investigated according to three dimensions—linguistic level (phonological, morphological, syntactic, lexical, semantic), linguistic task (comprehension, repetition, judgment, lexical access, propositioning), and linguistic unit (word, sentence, paragraph).

BAT consists of 32 subtests with individual scores for each. It includes *pointing, simple commands, verbal auditory discrimination, syntactic comprehension, naming, description, mental arithmetic,* etc. The collection of the native speaker's responses to the test items were imported from other countries by test administers who were also native speakers of the language.

Some of the data for the BAT Normative Study have been used to examine the relationship between age and language ability of normal elders because the data for BAT norm have been obtained from non-brain damaged participants with no known history of mental or neurological illness. For example, Juncos-Rabadán (1996) use Catalan, English, French, Galician, and Spanish data from the BAT Normative Study to examine the effects of age and education on the narratives of the elderly. For the details of the research done by Juncos-Rabadán (1996), see literature review in Chapter 2.

In the present research, the data are from the subtest of *description* in the Chinese BAT Normative Study and they are used for examining the impact of age on transitivity. These data originally belonged to the Normative Study of Bilingual Aphasia, and they were provided to the Pennsylvania State University several years ago. Now they are stored at the Pennsylvania State University. In this research, the data were used with permission. A detailed description of the subtest, *description*, appears later in the instrument section of this chapter. Also referenced is the other part related to the present study in the overall Chinese BAT. For example, references to the scores from a participant are obtained in another part of the subtest, such as naming or mental arithmetic when necessary.

4.3 Rationale for Using Secondary Chinese Data

The present research uses secondary Chinese data from the BAT Chinese Norm because it has four advantages. First, the data in present research can compare with the data in the previous research; thus, the results of the present research can compare with the previous research. Chinese data are relevant (but not repeated) to the previous research. In terms of content and elicitation method, the data in the present research follow the same or very similar criteria of the previous research. For example, the data in the present research follow the criteria of the research done by Juncos-Rabadán

(1994, 1996), Juncos-Rabadán and Iglesias (1994), Juncos-Rabadán, Pereiro and Rodríguez (2005), Makoni, Lin and Schrauf (2005). Therefore, the data in the present research are comparable to the data in the previous research, and the final results of present research can be reasonably compared to those of the previous research.

Second, new results can be found from the Chinese data. The Chinese data are different in language and/or language settings compared with the data from previous research. Also the Chinese data have not yet been analyzed or used for the present purpose of examining the impact of age on the elders' linguistic performances (with consideration of education). Something new can be found in a research when looking from a different angle (of language and/or language settings). New results can also be found when different linguistic aspects (transitivity processes) are examined in the Chinese data.

Third, the data are reliable for the present research. The Chinese data are collected systematically by qualified medical doctors following the criteria of BAT. (The names of the doctors are known; the name of the university in which the doctors work is also known.) And the results of data analyses for the Chinese BAT Norm are also known.

Fourth, the data are suitable to study how language is processed in the normal brain of Chinese speakers. This can be supported by Paradis, "The study of bilingual aphasia has also allowed researchers to better understand how language per se is represented and processed in the normal brain of monolingual speakers. (Paradis, 2004, p 63)" So the Chinese data from Chinese BAT norm are proper for studying the impact of age (brain aging) on linguistic aspects (transitivity processes) in the picture-elicited narratives of elderly Chinese speakers.

Because of these four strengths, the results of the present research on linguistic performance of the Chinese elders arising from the Chinese data can be compared with the results of previous research such as Juncos-Rabadán, et al. (1996, 2005) and Makoni, et al. (2005), and expand the scope of those researches.

4.4 Participants

The participants in this study consisted of 60 Chinese informants, 30 males and 30 females, whose ages range is from 50 to 79 years old, and they are recruited by Chinese medical doctors in Guangzhou in Guangdong Province in China. (The evidence is written in the Chinese data.) Their native language is Mandarin Chinese, and they have no known history of neurological or psychiatric illnesses, or other problems that might directly influence their storytelling performance, as required for this study. The preconditions for the participants to be chosen for BAT norms were that the participants had to be mentally normal, and the participants had to be in the country where the test language was spoken. According to Paradis (1987), the BAT is a quite reliable screening instrument, and thus, the analyses of the test results can show that the Chinese participants are non brain damaged, and have no mental or neurological illness.

According to the BAT Norms, 60 participants are sufficient. According to age, the 60 participants are divided into three groups: 50 to 59, 60 to 69 and 70 to 79. Each group has 20 participants, 10 males and 10 females. The education level of the participants is recorded in terms of formal education (school education).

The Chinese participants in the present research meet the criteria discussed in the above paragraph. And a summary of the specific information about their age and education appears in the following tables:

Table 4.4.1 The Participant's Age Information

Variable Age Groups		Age Mean	Age Standard Deviation	Median
Age groups	50—59	54.55	2.544	55.000
	60—69	64.85	2.254	65.000
	70—79	72.65	1.872	73.000

Table 4.4.2   The Participant's Education Information

Variable Age Groups		Education Mean	Education Standard Deviation	Median
Age groups	50—59	9.700	2.536	10.000
	60—69	6.800	1.881	6.000
	70—79	8.100	3.007	8.000

During the process of the data elicitation, the participants are asked to look at The Bird Nest Story pictures, a panel of six pictures from the Bilingual Aphasia Test (Paradis, 1987). Then the participants began to tell a bird nest story in Mandarin Chinese, and the story is recorded. The detailed description of the six pictures appears in the instrument section of this chapter. All the instructions were given in Chinese:"我将给你看一组六幅图片，这六幅图片组成一个故事。现在请看图并把这个故事讲给我。" (The meaning of the above Chinese characters translates as: "I'm going to show you a panel of six pictures; the pictures make a story. Now please look at the pictures and tell the story to me.")

4.5 Instrument

The panel of six pictures—The Bird Nest Story (Paradis, 1987) is used to elicit the narrative data. The reasons for selecting The Bird Nest Story are due to its content and least cultural orientation. The pictures tell a story about a man who climbed to a tree for a bird nest. The tree branch broke and the man fell down to the ground. He broke his leg and an ambulance took him to the hospital for treatment. The content of the pictures can be easily understood by normal elders. The pictures also intend to have as few cultural elements as possible. Paradis (1987) describes that "the story had to be as culturally neutral as possible." The Bird Nest Story is very different from The Building of a Snowman in that many places of the world have no snow and as a result, that "the building of a snowman" is not appropriate to some people when considering culture. Thus, The Bird Nest Story has been used in all languages in the BAT (only with the change of picture order or the dress of the girl according to some languages or religions).

The six pictures appeared in the subtest of *Description* in the BAT. And they were used to elicit spontaneous descriptions for answering Items 344 to 346 and for posttest analysis of Items 540 to 565 in the BAT. The six pictures appear in Figure 4.3 on the next page.

The series of the six pictures were used as the stimuli that can elicit a sequential story. The main points of the stimuli in the six pictures were summarized by Paradis (1987):

1. A girl points to a bird's nest in a tree. In the nest, a bird is feeding its young. A boy looks on.

2. While the girl is watching, the boy climbs into the tree and reaches for the nest. The bird is scared away.

3. The branch on which the boy is leaning breaks. The nest and the boy fall to the ground. The boy breaks his leg in the process.

4. While the boy with a broken leg lies near the fallen nest, the girl seeks help from a nearby house.

5. The boy is carried on a stretcher to an ambulance.

6. The boy is on a hospital bed with his leg in a cast, while his mother sadly looks on. Outside, the mother bird cries over the loss of her young.

Selected from Paradis 1987, p 117

Figure 4.5   The Bird Nest Story

4.6 Purpose of Analyzing the Picture-Elicited Narrative

This section explains the three purposes for analyzing the picture-elicited narratives which include two purposes for analyzing the narratives in the BAT, and one new purpose for analyzing the narratives for the present research. For the first purpose, in Items 344 to 346 in the BAT, the narrative elicited from The Bird Nest Story was analyzed to provide a preliminary, quick and clinical assessment of the participant. The items from 344 to 346 used in the BAT are in the following format:

344. Amount of speech: 0), 1) very little, 2) less than normal, 3) normal (344)

345. Did the patient go to the end?   +   -   (345)

346. Did the patient: 1) Simply describe the picture, 2) tell a connected story, 3) do neither?   (346)

Items 344 to 346 are used to represent a multiple-choice assessment of the patient's performance. The test administrator rates the narrative produced by the patient and provides scores. The scores reflect the amount of speech produced by the patient, the continuation of the story (whether the patient proceeded to the end) and the connections in the story (whether the patient told a connected story).

For the second purpose, the narrative elicited from The Bird Nest Story was analyzed to provide quantitative measures for the various components of the patients' verbal production in Items 540 to 565 in the BAT posttest. The complete analysis of the description narrative takes place after the BAT has been administered to the patient. The posttest analysis can provide an additional measure of fluency, accuracy and lexical diversity. For the details of Items 540 to 565, see Paradis (1987, p 192).

In the present study, the picture-elicited narratives are used for a new purpose: to analyze the participants' performance in transitivity to find the relationship between age and verbs across age groups. (The significance in so doing can be found in Chapter 1 of the present dissertation.)

4.7 Coding System

In order to analyze how elderly Chinese participants perform in the use of transitivity, a coding system is developed based on the main points of Paradis' stimuli with consideration to Chinese culture. The reason for developing the present coding system is because some components of the Chinese narratives are not covered or are neglected in the main points of Paradis' stimuli. For example, Chinese people like to talk about the relationship of the persons in the pictures. Chinese people would observe that the characters represent husband and wife or boy friend and girlfriend in the pictures. In order to take Chinese cultural aspects into account, the main points of Paradis' stimuli (in section 4.3) have been modified, and some items representing relational process and existential process have been added in the present research. In this way, the present coding system can reflect Chinese narratives. The present coding system involves all six different processes in transitivity and reflect the main Chinese narrative structure of 时间 (time), 地点 (location), 人物 (person), 事件或事件的过程, (event or the process of the event) and sometimes 评论 (comment) in Chinese although the study of the Chinese narrative structure is beyond the scope of this study.

Table 4.7 is a comparison of Paradis' stimuli and the coding system used in the present research:

Table 4.7   A Comparison of Paradis' Stimuli and Present Coding System

Picture1	Paradis' Stimuli (1987)	Present Coding System	Points
1	A girl points to a bird's nest in a tree. In the nest, a bird is feeding its young. A boy looks on.	1. There are two persons (a man and woman, or a boy and a girl, or loves) in the picture. 2. They are friends (boyfriend and girlfriend, lovers, or husband and wife, son and mom). 3. The (A) girl points to a bird's nest in a tree. 4. In the nest, a bird is feeding its young. 5. The (A) boy looks on.	5
2	While the girl is watching, the boy climbs into the tree and reaches for the nest. The bird is scared away.	1. While the girl is watching, 2. the boy climbs into the tree, 3. and reaches for the nest. 4. The bird is scared away.	4
3	The branch on which the boy is leaning breaks. The nest and the boy fall to the ground. The boy breaks his leg in the process.	1. The boy is leaning on the branch. 2. The branch breaks. 3. The nest and the boy fall to the ground. 4. The boy breaks his leg in the process.	4
4	While the boy with a broken leg lies near the fallen nest, the girl seeks help from a nearby house.	1. While the boy with a broken leg lies near the fallen nest, 2. the girl seeks help from a nearby house.	2
5	The boy is carried on a stretcher to an ambulance.	1. The boy is carried on a stretcher to an ambulance.	1
6	The boy is on a hospital bed with his leg in a cast, while his mother sadly looks on. Outside, the mother bird cries over the loss of her young.	1. The boy is on a hospital bed with his leg in a cast, 2. while his mother sadly looks on. 3. Outside, the mother bird cries over the loss of her young.	3

As noted from the table in the present coding system, the relational process is added. For example: *They are friends (boyfriend and girlfriend, lovers, or husband and wife, son and mom).* The existential process is also added; for example: *There are two persons (a man and a woman, or a boy and a girl, or lovers) in the picture.* In this way, the present coding system has all the six processes of transitivity described in Chapter 3, and the system can reflect the characteristics of the Chinese narratives at the same time.

4.8 Post-Explanation

The final section of this chapter explains and addresses some concerns for, or potential critiques of using the secondary data.

Some criticism about the Chinese data may exist. Since the Chinese data is secondary data collected for the normative purpose of the BAT, one critique is that these data were elicited by pictures, and thus, not "natural." Then the question is: what is "natural"? Even photos are sometimes considered unnatural because they reflect the choice and volition of the photographers. Absolute naturalness does not exist, and the study of Juncos-Rabadán (1994) supports that the BAT data can be used in the study of normal aging despite the question of naturalness.

Another critique of the picture-elicited narrative is the lack of interaction or something like a dialogue. Then the question is: What is a dialogue? And how long or how many words are required for a dialogue? Obviously, different types of interactions and dialogues exist. And the speeches in a dialogue made by one speaker can be either very short or very long since the speaker has the right to govern the length of a speech. The data were collected in the following way:

Doctor: Please look at the six pictures, and tell a story from the pictures.

(Then the elder tells a story while looking at the pictures.)

The Elder: One day, there are a man and a woman...

On the one hand, the task involves interaction and cooperation between the doctor and the elder; on the other hand, the response involves a rather long, independent answer. Since the research interest is to examine this kind of long independent speech by the elders, and since the research focuses on normal elders (no apparently neurological disorders), the data are useful according to suitability for the research purpose.

The third critique that arises is that the data are secondary. In practice, many researchers have used secondary data and have gained insights from the secondary data. For example, Makoni (2005) uses a significant amount of secondary data for analysis in his study of language and aging in an epidemiological study in New York City, and he find that some social biases which may arise when assessing older individuals can be overcome, particularly when interviewers and interviewees are matched for race and ethnicity. For details of Makoni's study, see Makoni (2005, pp 118-132). Therefore, secondary data can be used for a different research.

Chapter 5   ANALYSIS

Chapter 4 explained the methodology used to test this study's hypotheses. This chapter explains how data are processed and analyzed. Chapter 5 includes six sections: coding, rater training, rater's accuracy and reliability, transitivity, use of ANOVA, and the examples of data analysis.

5.1 Coding

Two raters (coders) coded all the narrative data according to the requirements of the coding sheet (for the coding system, see Chapter 4), which primarily follows the stimuli developed by Paradis (1987). An example of the Coding Sheet appears in Appendix A.

5.2 Coder Training

Both of the two raters are native Mandarin Chinese speakers. One is the author and the other is Mary (pseudonym), a PhD student with a master's degree in English language and literature from a Chinese university. The advantage of the author as a rater is the author's specialized familiarity with SFT. The author explained characteristics of transitivity to Mary and provided training for identifying material process, relational process, mental process, verbal process, behavioral process and existential process in transitivity. The training lasted two hours a day for three days. However, Mary could not distinguish the processes clearly, and sometimes became confused with different categories of transitivity. For example, Mary marked 看 (look) as a mental process, which in fact was a behavioral process. She complained of difficulty making distinctions due to very little knowledge about SFT. She said a long time would be necessary for her to study SFT. Teaching her SFT for an extended period was unrealistic since her available time was limited. The author changed coding strategy and asked her to find the Chinese words which appeared in the same or a similar context in the Coding Sheet (see Appendix A). Ultimately she was able to accurately find the Chinese words in all the coding sheets.

5.3 Raters Accuracy and Reliability

The accuracy of Mary was checked by the author, and the author's accuracy was checked by Mary. Since the present research contains 60 participants, and the linguistic items needed to be coded for each participant are 19 according to the Coding Sheet, altogether 1140 potential items needed to be coded. Of all the 1140 items (60×19), Mary accurately found 1131 items in the six categories of transitivity from the sixty participants' narratives. Her accuracy was 99.2 percent. The author accurately found 1133 items from all the 1140 items in the six categories of transitivity from the sixty participants' narratives; the author's accuracy was 99.3 percent (1133 out of 1140). This means that the author and Mary at least agreed on 1124 items of the total 1140; therefore the inter reliability of the two raters is equal to or more than 98.6 percent. The raters' accuracy and reliability can be seen in Figure 5.3.1 and Figure 5.3.2. The errors are made mainly due to the Chinese words that actually appear in transcriptions and the raters do not find them.

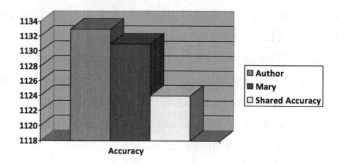

Figure 5.3.1   Two Raters' Accuracy and Inter-Accuracy

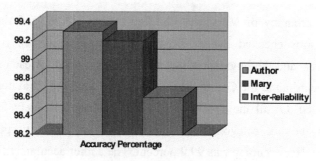

Figure 5.3.2   Two Raters' Reliability and Inter-Reliability

5.4 Transitivity

The transitivity that occurred in the Chinese elders' narratives was analyzed both by way of generalization (transitivity as a whole) and by way of specification (each process of transitivity). By generalization, the impact of age, education and gender on the participants' performances was analyzed in terms of the total number of transitivity processes (sum of all material, relational, mental, verbal, behavioral and existential processes) used by the participants in the narrative. By specification, the participants' performances were analyzed in a more detailed way by examining the impact of age, education and gender on the participants' performances in each of the six types of processes.

5.5 Analysis

The analyses of impacts of age, education and gender on the participants' performances in transitivity and its subcategories are very complicated and involve multiple factors and levels. For example, the present research includes three factors for data: age, education and gender. Age factor has three levels: A (age 50-59), B (age 60-69), and C (age 70-79); the education factor has three levels: L1 (3-6 years of education), L2 (7-9 years of education), and L3 (10-16 years of education). And because all these factors and levels can interact and impact the participant's performance in transitivity, and all the above multiple factors and levels need to be taken into account, the statistical analytical method, Analysis of Variance (ANOVA), was used to analyze the data to find which factor(s) and level(s) can have a statistically significant impact on the performance of transitivity. Specifically the general linear model (GLM) in ANOVA was used in the present research. Also the statistical software, Minitab®, was employed as an analysis tool. A further explanation of why and how GLM was used will be presented in Chapter 6.

The present research performed 7 analyses, using ANOVA to find significant factors and levels that can affect participants' performances in the transitivity and in the subcategories of transitivity:

Analysis 1 determined the impact of age, education and gender on the participants' overall performances of transitivity in all categories:

ANOVA: Age, Education and Gender vs. Overall Performances in All Categories of Transitivity:

(1) The impact of age

(2) The impact of education

(3) The impact of gender

(4) The impact of age and education

(5) The impact of age and gender

(6) The impact of gender and education

(7) The impact of age, education and gender

Analysis 2 determined the impact of age, education and gender on the participants' overall performances in the material process:

ANOVA: Age, Education and Gender vs. Overall Performances in Material Process:

(1) The impact of age

(2) The impact of education

(3) The impact of gender

(4) The impact of age and education

(5) The impact of age and gender

(6) The impact of gender and education

(7) The impact of age, education and gender

Analysis 3 determined the impact of age, education and gender on the participants' overall performances in the mental process:

ANOVA: Age, Education and Gender vs. Overall Performances in Mental Process:

(1) The impact of age

(2) The impact of education

(3) The impact of gender

(4) The impact of age and education

(5) The impact of age and gender

(6) The impact of gender and education

(7) The impact of age, education and gender

Analysis 4 determined the impact of age, education and gender on the participants' overall performances in the verbal process:

ANOVA: Age, Education and Gender vs. Overall Performances in Verbal Process:

(1) The impact of age

(2) The impact of education

(3) The impact of gender

(4) The impact of age and education

(5) The impact of age and gender

(6) The impact of gender and education

(7) The impact of age, education and gender

Analysis 5 determined the impact of age, education and gender on the participants' overall performances in the behavioral process:

ANOVA: Age, Education and Gender vs. Overall Performances in Behavioral Process:

(1) The impact of age

(2) The impact of education

(3) The impact of gender

(4) The impact of age and education

(5) The impact of age and gender

(6) The impact of gender and education

(7) The impact of age, education and gender

Analysis 6 determined the impact of age, education and gender on the participants' overall performances in the relational process:

ANOVA: Age, Education and Gender vs. Overall Performances in Relational Process:

(1) The impact of age

(2) The impact of education

(3) The impact of gender

(4) The impact of age and education

(5) The impact of age and gender

(6) The impact of gender and education

(7) The impact of age, education and gender

Analysis 7 determined the impact of age, education and gender on the participants' overall performances in the existential process:

ANOVA: Age, Education and Gender vs. Overall Performances in Existential Process

(1) The impact of age

(2) The impact of education

(3) The impact of gender

(4) The impact of age and education

(5) The impact of age and gender

(6) The impact of gender and education

(7) The impact of age, education and gender

5.6 Analyses with Extracts

The analysis of the data is a very complicated process and involves modifications made during the data analyzing process. The following explanation details the data analysis method with extracts, and explains the reasons for modifications made during analysis.

The data were transcribed, translated and analyzed in the following way. The style of the transcription is: Chinese characters followed by Chinese Romanization, word translation corresponding to a Chinese character, and an English sentence translation. The coding was completed by the raters according to the coding sheet in Appendix A. Then the analysis was made of the narrative. All these data's processing and analyses were exemplified by two extracts. Extract 1 was from Participant 4 (57 years old with 6 years of education) as an example since this narrative can reflected a kind of commonly used colloquial style and the imagination of the participant. Extract 1 from Participant 4 and Its Analysis:

1. 我　今天　看　了　这　张　图。　　　(Chinese characters)
   wǒ　jīntiān　kàn　le　zhè　zhāng　tú　　(Chinese Romanization)
   I　today　see　LE[①]　this　CL　picture　(Word by word translation)
   Today I see this picture.　　　　　(Sentence translation)
2. 他们　两　个肯　定　是　夫妻。

---

① This is the perfective tense marker in Mandarin Chinese.

tāmen liǎng gè kěn ding shìfūqī

they   two CL① sure   be couple

For sure they are husband and wife.

3. 他 们 俩 一起 在路上 走，看到   树上   有 一个 喜鹊。

tā men liǎ yìqǐ zài lù shang zǒu kàn dào shù shàng yǒu yí gè xǐquè

they two together on road walk see   tree up have one CL magpie

They walk together on the road and see that there is a magpie in the tree.

4. 喜鹊   会   叫， 喜鹊 哇里 哇啦 地   叫。

xǐquè   huì jiào, xǐquè wā lǐ wā lā de jiào

magpie can crow   magpie ONOMATOPOEIA②   crow

The magpie can crow.

5. 看   到 这 个 喜鹊 好 玩, 这 个 女 的 看 看 这个 喜鹊, 啊？

kàn dào zhè ge xǐquè hǎo wán zhè ge nǚ de kàn kan zhège xǐquèā

see   this CL magpie interesting this CL woman look look this CL

magpie

The woman sees the magpie. Ah, she feels the magpie is interesting.

6. 看 看 能 不 能 逮 到。

kàn kan néng bu néng dǎi dào

look look can BU③can   catch

She wants to know whether or not the man can catch the magpies.

7. 逮 到 了 就 上 去 看 一 看。

dǎi dào le jiù shàng qù kàn yī kàn

catch LE then up go have a look

To catch the magpies the man climbs up in the tree to have a look.

8. 这 个 女 的 就 站 在 边 上。

zhège   nǚ de jiù zhàn zài biān shang

this CL woman then stand at   side

The woman stands at side looking on.

---

① CL indicates the classifiers in Chinese.

② ONOMATOPOEIA indicates the onomatopoeias.

③ BU is the negative marker in Chinese.

9. 他　就　爬　了　上　去。
   tā jiù pá le shàng qù
   he then climb LE up go
   Then he climbs up in the tree.

10. 那　个　喜鹊　啦　飞　啦。
    nà ge xǐquè lā fēi lā
    that CL magpie LA[1] fly LA
    The magpie flies away.

11. 飞 了 以后 呢，小 雀 子 在 里面 哇里哇啦　　叫。
    fēi le yǐ hòu ne xiǎo què zǐ zài lǐmiàn wālǐwālā   jiào
    fly LE after NE[2] little bird in   ONOMATOPOEIA crow
    After the mother bird flies away, those little birds crow loudly in the
nest.

12. 就　　逮　那 个　小　雀子。
    jiù   dǎi nà ge xiǎo què zǐ
    then catch that CL little birds
    Then the man tries to catch those little birds.

13. 那　个 小　雀子 看 到 以后 都 慢　慢　跑。
    nà   ge xiǎo quèzǐ kàn dào yǐhòu dōu màn màn pǎo
    that CL little bird see then all slow slow run
    The little bird runs slowly when it sees this.

14. 一下　　跑 到 那 个　边　上　　呐，
    yíxià   pǎo dào nà ge biān shang nà
    all at once run to that CL edge on interjection
    It runs to the edge at once.

15. 快　　爬 到 那 个 边　上　的 时候，他　就 在 够。
    kuài pá dào nàge biān shang de shí hòu, tā jiù zài gòu
    nearly climb to that CL edge De[3] time, he then catch

---

① LA indicates the exemplifier "lā" in Chinese.
② NE indicates the onomatopoeia word "ne" in Chinese.
③ This is the adjectival marker or the special DE-structure marker in Mandarin Chinese which cannot
find counterparts in English.

At the time he nearly climbs to that edge, he begins to catch.

16. 这 个 女 的 叫 他 小 心 点，小 心 点，
    zhè ge nǚ de jiào tā xiǎo xīn diǎn, xiǎo xīn diǎn,
    this CL woman tell him carful, careful,
    This woman tells him to be careful, to be careful.

17. 没 有 讲 了几 句 话 啊①，
    méi yǒu jiǎng le jǐ jù huà ā
    not say Le several CL sentences interjection
    Not saying several sentences,

18. 他 这个 树 枝啊， 啪啦② 一下子 断了。
    tā zhège shù zhī ā, pālā yíxiàzi duàn le
    he this CL ranch interjection, ONOMATOPOEIA all at once break Le
    The branch breaks at once.

19. 唉③，断 了以后 呢，
    āi, duàn le yǐhòu ne
    interjection, break Le then NE
    Ah, after the branch breaks,

20. 那 个 树枝 下来了 掉在 地下，掉在 地下。
    nà ge shùzhī xiàlái le diào zài dìxià, diàozài dìxià
    that CL branch down Le fall to ground , fall to ground
    The branch falls down, falls down to the ground.

21. 这 个 小 雀子也掉 在 地下 来了。
    zhè ge xiǎo quèzǐ yě diào zài dì xià lái le
    this CL little bird too fall to ground come LE
    This little bird falls down to the ground, too.

22. 不 管 这个 小 雀子，先 抢救 这 个 人 要紧 了。
    bùguǎn zhège xiǎo quèzǐ xiān qiǎngjiù zhè gè rén yàojǐn le
    regardless this CL little bird, first rescue this CL man urgent Le

---

① An interjection usually used at the end of the sentence in Mandarin Chinese.
② ONOMATOPOEIA used to imitate the sound of breaking a branch of a tree.
③ An interjection in Mandarin Chinese.

To rescue the man is more urgent than to save the life of the little birds.

23. 把　这个　人　呢，群众　　出来　　看　了，
　　bǎ　zhè gè rén　ne qúnzhòng　chūlái　kàn le
　　ba this CL man NE　mass　come out look Le
　　The mass come out to see the man.

24. 打　　　电话　　打　　　电话。
　　dǎ　　diànhuà　dǎ　　diànhuà
　　make phone call make phone call
　　(Then) make a phone call (to the hospital).

25. 电话　　　离　这个　店　　还　很　远。
　　diànhuà　lí　zhège　diàn　hái hěn yuǎn
　　telephone away this CL De shop still very far
　　The telephone is far away from the shop.

26. 正　　好　　前面　来了　一　辆　小　汽车。
　　zhèng hǎo　qiánmian　lái le　yī liàng xiǎo qìchē
　　to the moment front　come LE one CL little　car
　　There comes a car in the front at the moment.

27. 她 说："同志，同志，　你 把　车　停一下。"
　　tā shuō tóngzhì tóngzhì nǐ bǎ　chē ting yí xià
　　she say comrade, comrade, you Ba① car stop a while
　　She said, "Comrade, Comrade, please stop your car for a while."

28. 这 个 司 机 很好，马 上 就 把 车 子 停 下 来。
　　zhè ge sījī hěn hǎo mǎshàng jiù bǎ chēzi ting xià lái②
　　this CL driver very nice at once then Ba car stop mimic word
　　This driver is very nice and stops the car at once.

29. 打　电话，在 医院　里。
　　dǎ diànhuà zài yīyuàn lǐ
　　make call with hospital in
　　And he makes a call to the hospital.

---

① A marker of direct object in Mandarin Chinese.
② Verb suffix indicating continuation, etc.

30. 医院　　马上　　派了　　救护车。
    yīyuàn　mǎshàng　pài le　jiùhùchē
    hospital　at once　send Le ambulance
    The hospital sends an ambulance immediately.

31. 在　　什么　地方，
    zài　shénme dìfāng
    in　what　place
    Where are they?

32. 我　说　在　临湖①吧。
    wǒ shuō zài línhú②ba
    I　say　at Linhu　ba
    I said they are at Linhu.

33. 把 车子 开 到 临湖　人　　很　多，
    bǎ chēzi kāi dào línhú　rén　hěn duō
    ba　car　drive to Linhu people very much
    Drive the car to Linhu where there are many people.

34. 就　把 这 个　人　带 到 车子　上，
    jiù　bǎ zhè gè rén　dài dào chēzi shàng
    then Ba this CL man take to　car　in
    Then (they) take the man into the car,

35. 带　　上　以后 就　带 到　医院。
    dài shàng　yǐhòu jiù　dài dào yīyuàn
    carry in　　after then take to hospital
    then they carry (the man) to the hospital.

36. 这个　　以后 呢，
    zhège　yǐhòu ne
    the affair then NE
    Then, and then,

---

① It indicates a place in the speaker's mind.
② It may be a name of a place in the narrator's mind.

37. 经过　　　　检查，　骨头　断　了。
jīngguò　　　jiǎnchá　gǔtou duàn le
experience examination bone break LE
After the examination, it is known that the bone is broken.

38. 医院　　给　他　　治疗。
yīyuàn　gěi　tā　　zhìliáo
hospital give him treatment
The hospital gives him a treatment.

39. 以后　　就　　　慢慢　地　好了。
yǐhòu　　jiù　　mànmàn de　hǎole
then right away　slowly　recovered
Then he recovers slowly after the treatment.

40. 这　一个　好像　是　夫妻　呢，
zhè　yígè hǎoxiàng　shì fū qī　ne
this one CL like　be couple NE
They are like a couple.

41. 在 服侍　他，在　照应　　他。
zài fúshì　tā　zài zhàoying　tā
in serving him in　take care him
The wife is taking care of him.

42. 对　着 这　张　　图　呢，
duì　zhe zhè zhāng　tú　ne
face ZHE　this CL picture NE
Seeing this picture,

43. 我　想起　我的　老婆，
wǒ　xiǎngqǐ wǒde lǎopó
I　think of my　wife
I think of my wife.

44. 不　知道　被　我　牵挂。
bú　zhīdào　bèi　wǒ qiān uà
not　know　passive I　miss

She does not know I am thinking of her.

Although this extract is a rather long narrative, it is used to demonstrate how the data are processed and analyzed. The total number of transitivity processes used is seven, according to the coding system. In Line 2, the word, "是"(are), is used to describe the relationship between the persons (husband and wife), and it meets the requirement for the environment in which the verb appears, so "是" (are) is accounted for, and it belongs to the relational process.

In Line 3, the word, "有" (there be), appears in the sentence "树上有一个喜鹊" (There is a magpie in the tree); the environment of "有" (there be) meets the requirement of the coding sheet which requires the meaning of "existence" in a certain environment. Thus, "有" (there be) is accounted for and it expresses the existential process. In Line 9, the word, "爬" (climb), in the sentence "他就爬了上去" (Then he climbs up in the tree) meets the requirement for the environment in which "爬" (climb) appears in the coding sheet; namely, it is the man who climbs in the tree, not the woman who climbs up in the tree. Thus, "爬" (climb) is accounted for in this case, and it expresses the material process.

In Line 18, the word, "断" (break), appears in the sentence "他这个树枝啊，啪啦一下子断了" (The branch breaks at once). The context of the word, "断" (break), meets the requirement of the coding sheet. Here, the branch of the tree breaks, not the trunk of the tree according to the pictures. Thus, "断" (break) is accounted for and it expresses the material process. In Line 20, the word, "掉" (fall), appears in the sentence "那个树枝下来了掉在地下，掉在地下" (The branch falls down, falls down to the ground). Thus, the environment of "掉" (fall) meets the requirement of the coding sheet, (but only one "掉" (fall) is accounted for since the second one is a repetition of the first one,) and it expresses the material process in this case.

In Line 27, the word, "说" (say), appeares in "她说:'同志，同志，你把车停一下' ". The context of "说" (say) meets the requirement for the environment in which it appears. The woman asks or seeks for help; thus, "说" (say) is accounted for, and it expresses the verbal process. In Line 37, the word, "断" (break), appears in the sentence of "骨头断了" (the bone is broken), and this context is similar to the context of the coding sheet: "the man breaks his leg in the process." Thus, "断" (break) is accounted for and it expresses the material process.

As far as each category of transitivity is concerned, the participant used four material processes, one verbal process, one relational process and one existential process. Notably, the transitivity and the categories of transitivity mentioned in this narrative only refer to those that meet the requirement of the coding sheet which was developed based on the coding system. To summarize the above analysis, the total number of transitivity processes used by this participant is seven.

Not all the processes of transitivity that appeared in the extract are counted for three reasons. First, some processes of transitivity are not required for the panel of six pictures of The Bird Nest Story, and although the processes appear in the narrative, they cannot be matched to the meaning in the coding system based on the stimulus developed by Paradis (1987). For example, in Line 3, the word, "走" (walk), appears in "他们俩一起在路上走" (They walk together on the road; "走" (walk) expresses the material process. However, no evidence shows that they walk together on the road in The Bird Nest Story pictures. In fact, the woman is the one who points to the birds nest in the tree; a mother bird is feeding her young. So, "走" (walk, material process expressing "process of doing") does not match any action in The Bird Nest Story pictures, and thus it should be ignored. In Line 24, the word, "打" (make) (expressing the material process), appears in "打 电 话, 打 电 话" (make a phone call, make a phone call). No telephone is present in the pictures and no evidence exists to show her "make a phone call." Thus, the word, "打" (make, material process), should be ignored.

Second, the repetition of some transitivity and the categories of transitivity create an impracticality for counting every verb that a participant uses in the narrative. For example, in Line 18, "断" (break) appeared in "他 这个树枝啊，啪啦一下子断了" (The branch breaks at once); in Line 19, the word, "断" (break), appears again in "断了以后呢" (after the branch breaks). Although the environment of "断" (break) meets the requirement of the coding sheet, the second word "断" (break) should be ignored since it is a repetition of the first use.

Third, counting each verb that expresses transitivity and the categories of transitivity is unrealistic. Previous experiments of trying to take every verb into account to analyze transitivity and the categories of transitivity resulted in a loss control. This is because the participants can say what they like to say even in front of the pictures used for elicitation. Some of the verbs are rather unrelated to the content of the pictures, and create confusion when trying to count every verb the participants narrated.

In order to take the various unrelated elements in the above extract into consideration, the same criteria should be used to evaluate each participant's performance in transitivity and in the sub-categories of transitivity. This means that only the part that meets the requirements will be considered. Thus, only the transitivity that corresponds with the coding system will be counted and coded on the coding sheet (in Appendix A). The detailed coding results for transitivity and each category of the transitivity will be shown in the next chapter together with results.

The result of the transitivity analysis is quite stable for participants from the same age group according to the coding system of the present research. The following narrative from Participant 1 (55 years old with 12 years of education) is relatively shorter than the narrative from Participant 4, yet the two participants have very similar results in terms of the analysis of the participant's performance in transitivity and the categories of transitivity. This is demonstrated in the following extract that provides another example of a narrative and its analysis.

Extract 2 from the transcription of Participant 1 and Its Analysis:

1. 这 树 上 有 一 窝 鸟。
   zhè shù shàng yǒu yī wō niǎo
   this tree on   have a nest bird
   There is a nest of birds in the tree.

2. 在 树 上 这 个 男 的,
   zài shù shàng zhè ge nán de
   on tree above this CL① man DE②
   This man is in the tree.

3. 这 个 女的 看 这 个 鸟 飞 下 来。
   zhè ge nǚ de kàn zhè ge niǎo fēi xià lái
   this CL woman see this CL bird fly down come
   This woman sees the bird flying down to the tree.

4. 在 树 上 这 个 窝 这 个 窝。
   zài shù shàng zhè ge wō zhè ge wō
   in tree above this CL nest this CL nest
   In the tree, the nest… the nest…

5. 这 个 大 鸟 没 食 吃, 就 喂 小 鸟 吃。
   zhè ge dà niǎo méi shí chī, jiù wèi xiǎo niǎo chī
   this CL big bird no food eat, then feed little bird eat
   The big bird has no food to eat; it feeds the little birds.

6. 这 个 树 上 有 一 个 窝,
   zhè ge shù shàng yǒu yí gè wō
   this CL tree above have one CL nest
   There is a bird nest in this tree,

7. 这 个 男 的 爬 上 树。
   zhè ge nán de pá shàng shù
   this CL man De climb in tree

----

① CL indicates the classifiers in Chinese.
② DE indicates the possessor marker in Chinese.

this man climbs into the tree.

8. 第　　三　图　树架　断　了，

dì　　sān　tú　shùjià　duàn　le

ordinal① third picture branch break LE

The third picture shows that the branch of the tree breaks.

9. 树架　断　了。

shùjià　duàn　le

branch break LE

The branch of the tree breaks.

10. 老　鸟　找　小　鸟，

lǎo niǎo　zhǎo　xiǎo niǎo

old bird look for little bird

The old bird looks for the little birds.

11. 人　掉　下　来　了。

rén　diào xià　lái　le

man fall down come LE

The man falls down from the tree.

12. 叫　救护车　来　着。

jiào jiù hù chē　lái　zhe

call ambulance come ZHE②

(She) calls the ambulance to come here.

13. 派　救护车　去　抢救，　抢救　呢。

pài　jiù hù chē　qù qiǎngjiù, qiǎngjiù ne

send ambulance　go first aid first aid Excl③,

The hospital sends an ambulance to give the man first aid.

14. 在　医院里 这 个 男 的 这 个 女 的 在 抢救。

zài yīyuàn lǐ　zhè ge nán de zhè ge nǚ de　zài qiǎngjiù

in hospital in this CL　man　this CL woman in emergency

---

① The dì is the marker for the ordinals (ordianal = dì cardinal) in Chinese.

② ZHE is the marker for the continuous tenses in Chinese.

③ Excl is short for the exclamation.

In the hospital, the man, (oh) the woman is giving emergency treatment.

15. 老　鸟　还　在　　找。

　　lǎo niǎo hái zài　　zhǎo

　　old bird still ZAI①look for

　　The old bird is still looking for (the little birds).

16. 这　个　小　鸟　跌　死　了。

　　zhè ge xiǎo niǎo diē sǐ　le

　　this CL little bird fall die ZHE

　　This little bird falls down to death.

17. 抢　救，　　　　这　个　腿　打　断　　了。

　　qiǎng jiù　　　　zhè ge tuǐ dǎ duàn le

　　emergency treatment this CL leg beat break LE

　　(He) is being given emergency treatment. The leg is broken.

　　In Line 1, the word, "有" (there be), appears in the sentence "这树上有一窝鸟" (there is a nest of birds in the tree). The environment of "有" (there be) meets the requirements of the context in the coding system; thus, "有" (there be) is counted, and it expresses an existential process in transitivity. In Line 5, the verb, "喂" (feed), appears in the sentence "这个大鸟没食吃，就喂小鸟吃" (The big bird has no food to eat; it feeds the little birds). It also meets the requirements of context for the verb. The participants are the big bird and small birds; the verb expresses the action of the big bird. Thus, the verb, "喂" (feed), is counted and it expresses a material process.

　　In Line 7, the verb, "爬" (climb), appears in the sentence "这个男的爬上树" (The man climbs in to the tree), and it meets the requirement of the context for the verb. The participant is the man, and the circumstance is the tree. Thus, the verb, "爬" (climb), is counted and it expresses a material process. In Line 8, the verb, "断" (break), appears in the sentence "第三图树架断了" (The third picture shows that the branch of the tree breaks). It meets

---

① ZAI is the marker for progressing of the action or state.

the requirement of the context in the coding system that expresses the breaking action of the branch. So the verb, "断" (break), is counted and it expresses a material process.

In Line 11, the verb, "掉" (fall), appears in the sentence "人掉下来了" (The man falls down from the tree). It meets the requirement for the context in the coding system. The participant is the man, and the action is "fall"; thus, it is counted, and it expresses a material process in transitivity. In Line 12, the verb, "叫" (call), appears in the sentence "叫救护车来着" (She calls the ambulance to come here). It meets the requirement of the context in the coding system. The woman asks (seeks) for help; thus, the verb, "叫" (call), is counted in this case, and it expresses a verbal process. In Line 17, the verb, "断" (break), appeared in the sentence, "这个腿打断了" (The leg is broken). The environment of "断" (break) meets the requirement of the coding sheet; it explains the fracture of the man's leg. Thus, "断" (break) is counted, and it expresses a material process.

However, the verb, "断" (break), in Line 9 is not counted because it is a repetition of the verb, "断" (break), in Line 8; the verb, "跌" (fall), in Line 16 (The little bird falls down to death) is not counted since this context is not required by the coding system. Here, the context is used to explain the old bird's action to express her sadness over the loss of her young.

To summarize, the total number of transitivity processes used in Extract 2 is seven, including five material processes, one verbal process and one existential process.

Comparisons can be made between Extract 1 and Extract 2 in terms of transitivity and each process of the transitivity. It is found that the transitivity used in Extract 1 is quite comparable to the transitivity used in Extract 2. The total number of transitivity processes used in Extract 1 and Extract 2 is the same: seven. A difference can be found in the categories of transitivity in the two extracts. Four material processes are used in Extract 1; five material processes are used in Extract 2. One relational process is used in Extract 1; no relational process is used in Extract 2. One verbal process is used in both

Extract 1 and Extract 2, and one existential process is used in both in Extract 1 and Extract 2.

Also revealed is that the difference in the number of transitivity processes used in the above two extracts is quite small although apparently a significant difference exists in terms of the length and participant's imagination displayed in the above two extracts. The possible reason for the same or very similar performance can be that age of the participants in the two extracts is in the same age group of 50 to 59; the first participant's age is 57 years old, and the second one's age is 55. Education does not seem to have an impact on the participants' performances in transitivity from that fact that the first one has 6 years of education and the second one has 12 years of education.

In the same way as the analysis of the data Extract 1 and Extract 2, all the sixty narratives from the sixty participants respectively were analyzed for transitivity and the sub-categories of transitivity according to the requirement in the coding sheet. The results of each participant's performance were marked and graded on the coding sheet. One hundred and twenty sets of coding sheets were used since each of the two raters used sixty sets of coding sheets. Then the results of the participants' performances were classified into different groups according to age, education and gender. In order to find the impact of age, (education and gender), on the performances of the participants in transitivity and each process of transitivity, the results were compared and further analyzed using ANOVA in terms of age, education and gender. The new results of the differences between the participants' performances in different groups appear in detail in Chapter 6, Results.

Chapter 6   RESULTS

Chapter 5 addressed the details of data processing and analysis which included coding, rater's training, rater's accuracy and reliability, transitivity, use of ANOVA, and the examples of data analysis. This chapter, based on ANOVA analysis, provides the research results of the impact of age, education and gender on the participants' performances in the aspects of transitivity and in each process of transitivity.

This chapter consists of nine sections. Section 1 is statistical solution which addresses the rationale of using General Linear Model (GLM) in ANOVA. In a sense, this section is an extension of Section 5.5 (Analysis) in Chapter 5, and it is a necessary extension which links analysis and research results. Section 2 is the analysis and results of the impact of age, education and gender on the overall performance of the participants in transitivity. Section 3 to Section 8 are the analysis and results of the impact of age, education and gender on the participants' performances in material, mental, verbal, behavioral, relational and existential processes, and Section 9 is a summary of the main results in this chapter.

6.1 Statistical Solution

The elements that can impact the participants' performances on transitivity are multiple and very complicated. Since each participant in the present research belongs to the three groups (age, education and gender) simultaneously, multiple variables are involved and their possible interaction aggravates the problem. Each factor has different levels. For example, the age group factor consists of three levels: A (50-59 years old), B (60-69 years old) and C (70-79 years old). The education factor also consists of three levels: L1 (3-6 years of education), L2 (7-9 years of education), L3 (10-16 years of education). For detailed factors and levels, see Table 6.1.

Table 6.1   Factors and Levels

Factor	Factor level		
Age Group	A (50-59 years old)	B (60-69 years old)	C (70-79 years old)
Education	L1 (3-6 years of education)	L2 (7-9 years of education)	L3 (10-16 years of education)
Gender	M (male)	F (female)	

The three factors with different levels interact with each other in the participant's overall performances in transitivity and in each of the six processes (material process, mental process, verbal process, behavioral process, relational process and existential process) within transitivity. All these factors and levels, rather than one single factor or level, can influence a given participant's performance simultaneously.

In order to take the interactions of the three factors with different levels into account, the statistical analytical method ANOVA (Analysis of Variance) was used to analyze the data to find which factor(s) and level(s) can have a statistically significant impact on the performance of transitivity. Also the statistical software, Minitab®, was employed as an analysis tool. Main effects plots help visually explain the factors' effects.

ANOVA was used to statistically determine whether or not the factors or their interactions significantly affected the subjects' use of transitivity. The ANOVA method is used to partition the total variation between the observation and the grand mean into the variation(s) due to the factor(s) and the variation due to error. If the variation due to the factor(s) is statistically large enough, then the factor(s) statistically affects (affect) the response; otherwise, if the variation due to the factor(s) is not statistically large enough, then factor(s) does (do) not statistically affect the response.

The P-value method is used to determine whether or not the results of the present research from the analysis are significant because the use of P-value method is more convenient than the traditional method that refers to F-test in the present research. P-value is defined as the smallest level of significance that will lead to the rejection of the null hypothesis, H_0, when the null hypothesis is actually true (Montgomery, 2002). A very small P-value (such as a significance level of 0.05 or lower) suggests that the sample results are unusual, and are significantly different from the null hypothesis. A large P-value (such as above a significance level of 0.05) suggests that the sample results are not unusual, and do not represent a significant difference from the null hypothesis. The P-value method and the traditional method (such as using F-test in ANOVA) are essentially the same; however, their decision criteria are different. The traditional method compares the test statistics to the critical value; whereas, the P-value method compares the significance level. However, the traditional method and P-value method are equivalent in the sense that they will always result in the same conclusion (Triola, 2000).

GLM in ANOVA is used instead of balanced ANOVA in the analysis because the design is not balanced. A balanced design is one with equal numbers of observations at each combination of the treatment levels. In this research, the design is not balanced. For example, the education level L1 and L3 have 21 observations respectively, while education level L2 has 18 observations. Thus, a general linear model is used in the analysis.

When a factor is quantitative with three or more levels, partitioning the sums of squares from that factor into effects of polynomial orders is appropriate. If the factor has k levels, the sums of squares can be partitioned into k-1 polynomial orders (Levene, 1960). In this research, however, all the three factors, age group, education and gender are categorical (qualitative). Thus, the order is 1 for all the qualitative factors in the linear model.

In ANOVA, using a general linear model, sequential (Type I) sums of squares and adjusted (Type III) sums of squares are the output from Minitab®. Adjusted (Type III) sums of squares are used by Minitab® by default for all

GLM calculations. Adjusted sums of squares are the additional sums of squares determined by adding each particular term to the model, given that the other terms are already in the model. Sequential sums of squares are the sums of squares added by a term with only the previous terms entered in the model. Sequential sums of squares can be different for the same factor when the design is unbalanced or if covariates exist.

Covariates are random variables treated as concomitants (Concomitant Variable: an incidental or subordinate variable in statistics) or as other influential variables that also affect the response. Covariates in Design of Experiments (DOE) are uncontrolled variables that influence the response but do not interact with any of the other factors being tested at the time. Therefore, if they are present during the experiment, then they would show as measurements of error (Isixsigma, 2004).

In an unbalanced design or a design involving covariates, GLM's sequential sums of squares (the additional model sums of squares explained by a variable) will depend upon the order in which variables enter the model. The subsequent order of fitting is the order of terms in the model. The sequential sums of squares for unbalanced terms X_1 X_2 will be different depending upon the order that they are entered in the model. The default adjusted sums of squares (sums of squares with all other terms in the model), however, will be the same, regardless of model order (Minitab®, 2000) (Draper, 1998). Usually, adjusted sums of squares are used. In the research, no covariate is involved.

Adjusted mean square (Adj MS) is adjusted sums of squares divided by its corresponding degree(s) of freedom. F (F test) in ANOVA is equal to adjusted mean square due to factor divided by adjusted mean square due to error. When using F in ANOVA, α-value (or level of significance, α = Probability [reject null hypothesis H_0 | H_0 is true]) needs to be given to arrive at a conclusion. Thus, the conclusion will depend on the α-value given in advance. However, the P-value method is much more convenient to use in practice; it does not need the α-value. Therefore, the P-value method was used in the present research.

6.2 Impact of Age, Education and Gender on the Participants' Overall Performance of Transitivity

The overall performance of transitivity is determined by the total points a participant received in the coding sheet, which is the sum of performance for material, mental, verbal, behavioral, relational and existential processes. For example, the 20th participant scored 5 points in material process (scored 5 point in material process means 5 material processes were used), 0 points in mental process, and 1 point in verbal process, 1 point in behavioral process, 1 point in relational process and 1 point in existential process: the total points for the 20th participant are 9, which are marked in yellow in Table 6.2.1. The details of this participant's performance appear in Table 6.2.1.

Table 6.2.1 The 20th Participant's Transitivity Performance

Coding Sheet*

标号：_____

NO: ___20___

请仔细阅读每一段叙述，并在下面标出你能在每一段叙述中找到的粗体动词。要求叙述中的动词出现的环境与下面相同或相近。

Please read each narrative carefully, and mark out the following blackened verbs which you could find in each narrative. The verbs appear in the narrative should be the same as or similar to what they appear in the following context.

1. 图中**有**两个人（一个男人和一个女人/一个男孩和一个女孩/一对夫妻/恋人）。

(6**)

There **are** two persons (a man and a woman / a boy and a girl /husband and wife/ lovers) in the picture.

2. 他们**是**一对恋人（一个男人和一个女人/一个男孩和一个女孩/一对夫妻/恋人/ 儿子和母亲）。

(5)

They **are** friends (a man and a woman /a boy and a girl / husband and wife/ lovers / son and mom).

3. 一个女孩 (一个女的/那个女的/那个女人) 指着树上的一个鸟巢。   (1)

A girl (a female / the woman / the lady) **points** to a bird nest in a tree.

4. 在鸟巢里，一只鸟在喂小鸟。   (1)

In the nest, a bird is **feeding** its young.

5. 一个男孩(一个男人)在看。   (4)

A boy (a man) **looks** on.

6. 那个女孩 (那个女的/那个女的/那个女人) 在看，   (4)

While the girl（the female/ the woman/ the lady）is **watching**,

7. 那个男孩(那个男的/那个男的/那个男人) 爬上树，   (1)

the boy (the male/ the man/ that man) **climbs** into the tree,

8. 接近(爬向)了鸟巢。   (1)

and **reaches** for the nest.

9.（大/老）鸟吓走了。   (2)

The (big/ old) bird is **scare**d away.

10. 那个男孩(那个男的/那个男的/那个男人)依在树枝上。   (4)

The boy (the male/ the man/ that man) is **leaning** on the branch.

11. 树枝断了。   (1)

The branch **breaks**.

12. 鸟巢和那个男孩(那个男的/那个男的/那个男人)掉在地上。   (1)

The nest and the boy (the male/ the man/ that man) **fall** to the ground.

13. 在这过程中，男孩(男的/那个男的/那个男人)摔断了腿。   (1)

The boy (the male/ the man/ that man) **breaks** his leg in the process.

14. 那个男孩(那个男的/那个男的/那个男人)躺在掉下来的鸟巢附近，   (4)

While the boy (the male/ the man/ that man) **lies** near the fallen nest,

15. 那个女孩(那个女的/那个女的/那个女人)到附近请（寻）求帮助。   (3)

the girl（the female/ the woman/ the lady）**seeks (asks)** help from a nearby house.

16. 那个男孩(那个男的/那个男的/那个男人)被用担架抬上了救护车。   (1)

The boy (the male/ the man/ that man) is **carried** on a stretcher to an ambulance.

17. 那个男孩(那个男的/那个男的/那个男人)躺在医院的床上，腿上打着石膏。   (4)

The boy (the male/ the man/ that man) is **lying** on a hospital bed with his leg in a cast.

18. 他母亲（那个女孩/那个女的/那个女的/那个女人)悲伤地**看**着他。   (4)

His mother (the girl /the female/ the woman/ the lady) sadly **looks** on.

19. 鸟妈妈(大鸟/老鸟/母鸟)在外面因为她孩子的死而**哭**。   (4)

Outside, the mother bird (the big bird / the old bird / the female bird) **cries** over the loss of her young.

* 1 and 2 have been added, 14, 15 and 18 have been modified.

** Code for transitivity.

In the above table, the number in the parentheses is a code for transitivity: 1 represents material process; 2 represents mental process; 3 represents verbal process; 4 represents behavioral process; 5 represents relational process, and 6 represents existential process.

As noticed previously that the 20th participant scored 0 point in mental process, 1 point in verbal process, 1 point in behavioral process, 1 point in relational process and 1 point in existential process. Small numbers such as 0, 1 (or 2) appeared. However, the small numbers will not affect the reliability of the significance of the tests. For instance, 0 itself is a number; it means the participant's performance is 0 in the present research, but it does not mean the performance is unknown, and unknown performance can be, in fact, any number. So the argument is: if more than 95 percent of the participants' performances in a specific item are 0, this item is still reliable in the sense that the participants' 0 performances are normal while the performances other than 0 are abnormal, and an investigation should be conducted. For instance, a participant's performance is not 0 in an item which should be 0, the participant should be given special attention, something can be wrong with the participant, in this sense, and the item can have a diagnostic function. Another instance is that a specific item required appearing only once in a certain context will be wrong or problematic if its appearance is any number other than 1. Number itself, no matter small or big, has its own meaning. And one cannot expect that transitivity processes will be evenly distributed in a given context.

The results indicate that age can have a significant impact on the overall performance of transitivity between the three age groups (50-59, 60-69 and 70-79). In Table 6.2.2, the P-value for the age group is 0.040, and the P-value is small (less than 0.05, significance level) and sufficient to contend that age group is statistically significant to affect the level of the participants' overall performance in transitivity.

Table 6.2.2   General Linear Model: Overall Transitivity versus Age Group, Education and Gender

Factor	Type	Levels	Values
Age Group	fixed	3	A, B, C
Education	fixed	3	L1, L2, L3
Gender	fixed	2	F, M

Analysis of Variance for Overall transitivity, Using Adjusted SS for Tests

Source	DF	Seq SS	Adj SS	Adj MS	F	P
Age Group	2	24.133	25.478	12.739	3.48	0.040
Education	2	2.345	7.685	3.842	1.05	0.359
Gender	1	2.863	1.163	1.163	0.32	0.576
Age Group*Education	4	24.295	23.346	5.837	1.60	0.193
Age Group*Gender	2	1.815	0.076	0.038	0.01	0.990
Education*Gender	2	6.435	6.341	3.171	0.87	0.428
Age Group*Education*Gender	4	12.613	12.613	3.153	0.86	0.495
Error	42	153.683	153.683	3.659		
Total	59	228.183				

DF: Degree of Freedom; Seq SS: Sequential Sums of Squares; Adj SS: Adjusted Sums of Squares; Adj MS: Adjusted Mean of Squares; F: Adj MS due to factor / Adj MS due to error; P: P-value

The present study found that the points of participants' performances increase from Age Group 50-59 to Age Group 60-69, and the points of participants' performances decrease from Age Group 60-69 to Age Group 70-79. The tendency of the age group's performance in transitivity is like a

"∧" shape as shown in Figure 6.2.1. Therefore, the performance of Age Group 60-69 in transitivity is higher than that of Age Group 50-59 and Age Group 70-79 respectively; the performance of Age Group 60-69 in transitivity is the highest among the three age groups. Thus, in terms of performances in transitivity, Age Group 60-69 can be called golden age group. The performances of Age Group 50-59 are similar to Age Group 70-79 in transitivity, or performance of Age Group 70-79 is at least not lower than the performance of Age Group 50-59 in transitivity. See Table 6.2.2 and Figure 6.2.1.

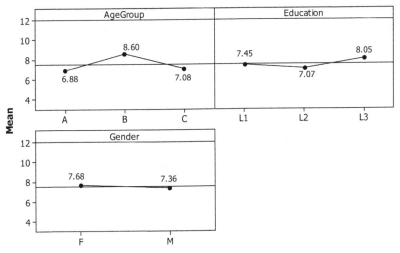

Figure 6.2.1   Main Effects plot upon Overall Transitivity

The present research result is partially contradictory to the impact of age in previous research by Juncos-Rabadán, Pereiro and Rodríguez (2005) that suggested aging reduces density of informational content (the density of information refers to the content appropriate nest based on the Bird Story Pictures). The current study also contradicts the result of Juncos-Rabadán (1996) who reported the ability to understand and tell stories declines with increasing age regardless of language. The ability to understand and tell stories can also refer to the content appropriateness the Bird based on Story Pictures, and the content can be expressed through transitivity. The present research results indicate that age impact on the performance of the elderly is not a simple process of declination, but rather a complex process or dual process which involves an increase from Age Group 50-59 to Age Group 60-69, and then a decrease from Age Group 60-69 to Age Group 70-79.

Education does not have a significant impact on the overall performance of transitivity between the three age groups (50-59, 60-69 and 70-79). P-value is equal to 0.359 (Table 6.2.2), which is larger than 0.05. The present research also reflects, in Figure 6.2.1, that educational level is statistically unrelated to the age groups' performances. So this result is contrary to previous research (Juncos-Rabadán, 1996) suggesting education increases capacity to tell stories, but the current study agrees with the assumptions of Makoni, Lin and Schrauf (2005) that education does not affect the performance of elders in picture elicited narratives.

Gender does not have a significant impact on the overall performance of transitivity between the three age groups (50-59, 60-69 and 70-79). P-value is equal to 0.576 (Table 6.2.2) which is far above 0.05. Also Figure 6.2.1 indicates no difference in the performance of overall transitivity between genders.

The main effects plot of age group, education and gender upon the participants' overall performances in transitivity is shown in Figure 6.2.1. The main effects plot displays the response means for each factor level. A horizontal line, called the reference line, represents the grand mean of the response data in the main effects plot. The effects are the differences between the means and the reference line. The main effects plot is often used to compare magnitudes of main effects. In this case, the effects of age group upon the participants' overall performances in transitivity are larger compared to the effects of education and gender. The effects of education upon the participants' overall performances in transitivity are larger compared to the effects of gender. Age group significantly affects the participants' overall performances in transitivity. Education and gender do not statistically significantly affect the participants' overall performances in transitivity.

As for the interactions between age, education and gender with different levels in each of them, the present research results show that these interactions do not have significant impacts on the participants' overall performances of transitivity. The P-value for the interactions between age and education is 0.193 (Table 6.2.2). This value is large (larger than P = 0.05) enough to say that no interaction between age group and education exists. The interactions of other pairs (age and gender with P = 0.990, education and gender with P = 0.428) do not have significant impacts on the participants' overall performances in transitivity. The P-value for the interactions of age, gender and education is 0.495, so the interactions of age, gender and education as a whole do not have a statistically significant effect on the participants' overall performances in transitivity. Figure 6.2.2 shows that the interactions of age, education and gender do not exist.

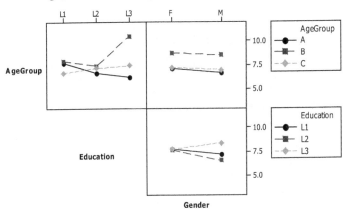

Figure 6.2.2   Interactions Plot upon Overall Transitivity

6.3 Impact of Age, Education and Gender on Material Process

Material process is a major component in transitivity, and it models the experiences of "happening and doing." Of all the 60 participants, each participant's overall performance on material process was identified by the two coders. For example, the points assigned to of the 42nd participant's material process are 6. Table 6.3.1 shows the details of how the material processes were used by the 42nd participant and how they were marked by the coders.

Table 6.3.1   The 42nd Participant's Material Process Performance

标号：_____ NO: __42__ 请仔细阅读每一段叙述，并在下面标出你能在每一段叙述中找到的粗体动词。要求叙述中的动词出现的环境与下面相同或相近。 Please read each narrative carefully, and mark out the following blackened verbs which you could find in each narrative. The verbs appear in the narrative should be the same a or similar to what they appear in the following context.

3. 一个女孩(一个女的/那个女的/那个女人)**指**着树上的一个鸟巢。   (1)

   A girl (a female / the woman / the lady) **points** to a bird's nest in a tree.

4. 在鸟巢里，一只鸟在**喂**小鸟。   (1)

   In the nest, a bird is **feeding** its young.

7. 那个男孩(那个男的/那个男的/那个男人)**爬**上树，   (1)

   The boy (the male/ the man/ that man) **climbs** into the tree,

8. **接近**(爬向)了鸟巢。   (1)

   and **reaches** for the nest.

11. 树枝**断**了。   (1)

   The branch **breaks**.

12. 鸟巢和那个男孩(那个男的/那个男的/那个男人)**掉**在地上。   (1)

   The nest and the boy (the male/ the man/ that man) **fall** to the ground.

13. 在这过程中，男孩(男的/男的/男人)**摔断**了腿。   (1)

   The boy (the male/ the man/ that man) **breaks** his leg in the process.

16. 那个男孩(那个男的/那个男的/那个男人)被用担架**抬**上了救护车。   (1)

   The boy (the male/ the man/ that man) is **carried** on a stretcher to an ambulance.

Table 6.3.1 shows that the 42nd participant's use of material process is construed through the verbs, 指 **(point)**, 爬 **(climb)**, 断 **(break)**, 掉 **(fall)**, 摔断 **(break)**, and 抬 **(carry)**.

The present research results indicate that age does not have a significant impact on the participants' overall performances in the material process in transitivity among the three age groups (50-59, 60-69 and 70-79). P-value is equal to 0.418 which is far above P = 0.05. See Table 6.3.2. So no statistical difference in the performances in material process among the three age groups exists. This is contradictory to the results of the study of Juncos-Rabadán, Pereiro and Rodríguez (2005) that indicates that aging reduces density of informational content.

Table 6.3.2   General Linear Model: Material Process versus Age Group, Education, Gender

Factor	Type	Levels	Values
Age Group	fixed	3	A, B, C
Education	fixed	3	L1, L2, L3
Gender	fixed	2	F, M

Analysis of Variance for Material Process, Using Adjusted SS for Tests

Source	DF	Seq SS	Adj SS	Adj MS	F	P
Age Group	2	3.033	3.560	1.780	0.89	0.418
Education	2	1.415	3.012	1.506	0.75	0.477
Gender	1	0.047	0.003	0.003	0.00	0.968
Age Group*Education	4	5.962	6.692	1.673	0.84	0.509
Age Group*Gender	2	0.438	0.035	0.018	0.01	0.991
Education*Gender	2	1.697	0.828	0.414	0.21	0.813
Age Group*Education*Gender	4	6.541	6.541	1.635	0.82	0.520
Error	42	83.850	83.850	1.996		
Total	59	102.983				

DF: Degree of Freedom; Seq SS: Sequential Sums of Squares; Adj SS: Adjusted Sums of Squares; Adj MS: Adjusted Mean of Squares; F: Adj MS due to factor/Adj MS due to error; P: P-value

In the present study, a trend appears, which coincides with the overall participants' performances on the overall transitivity in the previous section: the performance of Age Group 60-69 in material process is better than that of Age Group 50-59 and Age Group 70-79, and the performance of Age Group 50-59 in material process is similar to Age Group 70-79. Age Group 60-69's performance in material process is the highest among the three age groups. Figure 6.3.1 shows the differences among the three age groups.

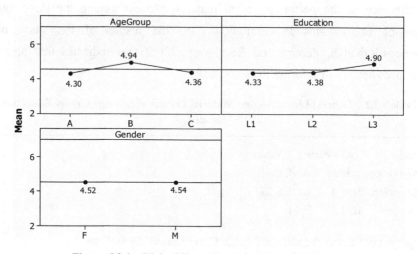

Figure 6.3.1   Main Effects Plot upon Material Process

However, these differences mentioned in the previous paragraph are too small to be counted because of the P-value in Table 6.3.2.

Education does not have a significant impact on the participants' performances in material process among the three age groups (50-59, 60-69 and 70-79). P-value is equal to 0.477, which is far above P=0.05. See Table 6.3.2 and Figure 6.3.1.

Gender does not have a significant impact on the participants' performances in material process among the three age groups (50-59, 60-69 and 70-79). P is equal to 0.968 (Table 6.3.2) which is larger than P=0.05. Also Figure 6.3.1 indicates no difference in the participants' performances in material process between genders; actually the two gender groups performed quite similarly. See Table 6.3.2 and Figure 6.3.1.

The main effects plot of age group, education and gender upon material process appears in Figure 6.3.1. In this case, the effects of age group upon material process are larger compared to the effects of education although both of them do not have a statistically significant effect on the participants' performances in material process. Also, the effects of education upon the participants' performances in material process are larger compared to the effects of gender.

As for the interactions between age, education and gender, the smallest P-value that appears in the interaction pair of age and education is 0.509. It is large (larger than 0.05 significance level) enough to indicate no interaction exists between age group and education, or the interaction of age and education does not have a significant impact on the participants' performances in material process in the transitivity. For the same reason, the interactions of other pairs (age and gender with P=0.991, education and gender with P=0.813) do not have on any significant impact on the participants' performances in material process in transitivity. The interactions of age, education and gender as a whole do not have a statistically significant impact on the participants' performance in material process in transitivity (P= 0.520).

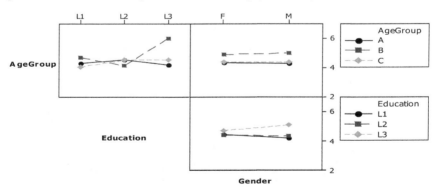

Figure 6.3.2   Interactions Plot upon Material Process

6.4 Impact of Age, Education and Gender Impact on Mental Process

The mental process is also a major component in transitivity, and it models the experiences of "sensing: feeling, thinking, and perceiving." Of all the 60 participants, each participant's overall mental process performance was identified by the two coders. For example, the point representing the 18th participant's mental process performance is 1. Table 6.4.1 shows the details of how the 18th participant used the mental process and how the mental process was identified by the two coders. The verb, 吓 (**scare**), was used by the 18th participant.

Table 6.4.1   The 18th Participant's Mental Process Performance

标号：＿＿＿＿＿ NO:＿＿＿18＿＿＿ 请仔细阅读每一段叙述，并在下面标出你能在每一段叙述中找到的粗体动词。要求叙述中的动词出现的环境与下面相同或相近。 Please read each narrative carefully, and mark out the following blackened verbs which you could find in each narrative. The verbs appear in the narrative should be the same as or similar to they appear in the following context. 9.（大/老）鸟吓走了。   (2) 　　The (big/ old) bird is **scared** away.

As for the participants' mental process performance in transitivity, age does not have a significant impact among the three age groups (50-59, 60-69 and 70-79). P is equal to 0.349, which is far above P = 0.05 as shown in Table 6.4.2. No difference exists for the mental process performance among the three age groups. This is also contradictory to the results of Juncos-Rabadán, Pereiro and Rodríguez (2005) who suggest that aging reduces density of informational content. Although a trend appears which coincides with the participants' overall performance in the overall transitivity: the mental process performance of Age Group 60-69 is better than that of Age Group 50-59 and Age Group 70-79, and the mental process performance of Age Group 50-59 is similar to that of Age Group 70-79, these differences cannot be considered because of the P-value in Table 6.4.2.

Table 6.4.2   General Linear Model: Mental Process versus Age Group, Education, Gender

Factor	Type	Levels	Values
Age Group	fixed	3	A, B, C
Education	fixed	3	L1, L2, L3
Gender	fixed	2	F, M

Analysis of Variance for Mental Process, Using Adjusted SS for Tests

Source	DF	Seq SS	Adj SS	Adj MS	F	P
Age Group	2	0.10000	0.20115	0.10058	1.08	0.349
Education	2	0.54592	0.44545	0.22272	2.39	0.104
Gender	1	0.00647	0.04873	0.04873	0.52	0.474
Age Group*Education	4	0.17494	0.14032	0.03508	0.38	0.824
Age Group*Gender	2	0.14207	0.26453	0.13227	1.42	0.253
Education*Gender	2	0.02928	0.02477	0.01239	0.13	0.876
Age Group*Education*Gender	4	0.48465	0.48465	0.12116	1.30	0.286
Error	42	3.91667	3.91667	0.09325		
Total	59	5.40000				

DF: Degree of Freedom; Seq SS: Sequential Sums of Squares; Adj SS: Adjusted Sums of Squares; Adj MS: Adjusted Mean of Squares; F: Adj MS due to factor/Adj MS due to error; P: P-value

Education does not have a significant impact on the participants' mental process performance in transitivity among the three age groups (50-59, 60-69 and 70-79). P is equal to 0.104, which is larger than P=0.05. See Table 6.4.2.

Gender does not have a significant impact on the participants' mental process performance in transitivity among the three age groups (50-59, 60-69 and 70-79). P is equal to 0.474 which is larger than P = 0.05. See Table 6.4.2.

The main effects plot of age group, education and gender upon the participants' mental process performances in transitivity appears in Figure 6.4.1. In this case, although all of them do not have a statistically significant effect on the mental process performance in transitivity, the effects of age group upon the mental process performance in transitivity are larger than the effects of gender; the effects of education upon the mental process performance are larger than the effects of gender.

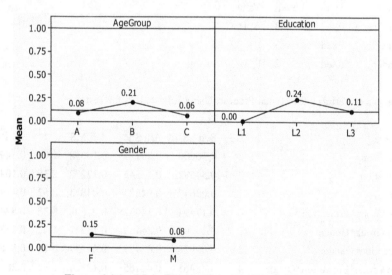

Figure 6.4.1   Main Effects Plot upon Mental Process

As for the interactions between age, education and gender, the smallest P-value, 0.824 (see Table 6.4.2), appears in the interaction pair of age and education. This value is larger than P = 0.05. Thus, the interaction of age and education does not play a significant role in the participants' mental process performance in transitivity. The interactions of other pairs (age and gender with P = 0.253, education and gender with P = 0.876) do not have a significant impact on the participants' mental process performances in transitivity; the interactions of age, education and gender as a whole do not, statistically, have a significant impact on the participants' mental process performances in transitivity (P = 0.286). See Table 6.4.2 and Figure 6.4.2.

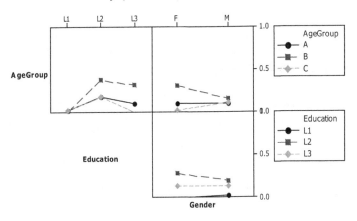

Figure 6.4.2   Interactions Plot upon Mental Process

6.5 Impact of Age, Education and Gender on Verbal Process Performances

Verbal process is a type of transitivity, and it models the experiences of "saying." Of all the 60 participants, each participant's overall verbal process performance was identified by the two coders. For example, the point for the 9th participant's verbal process performance is 1. Table 6.5.1 shows the details of how the 9th participant used the verbal process and how the verbal process was identified by the two coders. The verb, 求 **(seek, ask)**, was used by the 9th participant.

The results show that age does not have a significant impact on the participants' verbal process performances in transitivity among the three age groups (50-59, 60-69 and 70-79). P is equal to 0.992 which is larger than P = 0.05. See Table 6.5.2. Thus, no statistically significant difference in the participants' verbal process performance appears among the three age groups.

Table 6.5.1　The 9th Participant's Verbal Process Performance

标号：＿＿＿＿＿＿＿

NO:　　　9

请仔细阅读每一段叙述，并在下面标出你能在每一段叙述中找到的粗体动词。要求叙述中的动词出现的环境与下面相同或相近。

Please read each narrative carefully, and mark out the following blackened verbs which you could find in each narrative. The verbs appear in the narrative should be the same or similar as they appear in the following context.

15. 那个女孩(那个女的/那个女的/那个女人)到附近**请（寻）求**帮助。　　　　(3)

　　The girl (the female/ the woman/ the lady) **seeks (asks)** help from a nearby house.

Table 6.5.2　General Linear Model: Verbal Process versus Age Group, Education, Gender

Factor	Type	Levels	Values
Age Group	fixed	3	A, B, C
Education	fixed	3	L1, L2, L3
Gender	fixed	2	F, M

Analysis of Variance for Verbal Process, Using Adjusted SS for Tests

Source	DF	Seq SS	Adj SS	Adj MS	F	P
Age Group	2	0.1000	0.0033	0.0017	0.01	0.992
Education	2	1.1561	0.9930	0.4965	2.25	0.117
Gender	1	0.0298	0.0048	0.0048	0.02	0.883
Age Group*Education	4	2.0239	1.9621	0.4905	2.23	0.082
Age Group*Gender	2	0.2380	0.1095	0.0547	0.25	0.781
Education*Gender	2	0.8450	0.8549	0.4274	1.94	0.156
Age Group*Education*Gender	4	0.7571	0.7571	0.1893	0.86	0.496
Error	42	9.2500	9.2500	0.2202		
Total	59	14.4000				

DF: Degree of Freedom; Seq SS: Sequential Sums of Squares; Adj SS: Adjusted Sums of Squares; Adj MS: Adjusted Mean of Squares; F: Adj MS due to factor/Adj MS due to error; P: P-value

This is contradictory to the results of Juncos-Rabadán, Pereiro and Rodríguez (2005) who argued that aging reduces density of informational content. From Figure 6.5.1, all the three age groups performed very similarly in the verbal process in transitivity. Figure 6.5.1 is on the next page.

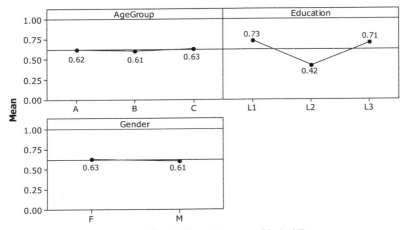

Figure 6.5.1   Main Effects Plot upon Verbal Process

Education does not have a significant impact on the participants' verbal process performances in transitivity among the three age groups (50-59, 60-69 and 70-79). P is equal to 0.117, which is larger than P = 0.05. Although education apparently had an impact on the participants' performances among the three groups (Figure 6.5.1), the impact was too small to be considered significant due to the P-value (0.117).

Gender does not have a significant impact on the participants' verbal process performances in transitivity among the three age groups (50-59, 60-69 and 70-79). P is equal to 0.883, which is larger than P = 0.05.

The main effects plot of age group, education and gender upon the participants' verbal process performances in transitivity appears in Figure 6.5.1. In this case, the effects of education upon the verbal process performance in transitivity are larger than the effects of age and gender, although all of them do not have a statistically significant effect on the participants' verbal process performances in transitivity.

As for the interactions among age, education and gender, the smallest P-value appears in the interaction pair of age and education in which the P-value is 0.082. See Table 6.5.2. This value is larger than P = 0.05. Thus, the interaction of age and education does not have a significant impact on the participants' verbal process performances in transitivity. The interactions of other pairs (age and gender with P = 0.781, education and gender with P=0.156) do not have a significant impact on the participants' verbal process performances in transitivity. The interactions of age, education and gender, as a whole, do not, statistically, have a significant impact on the participants' verbal process performances in transitivity (in this case, P= 0.496). See Table 6.5.2 and Figure 6.5.2.

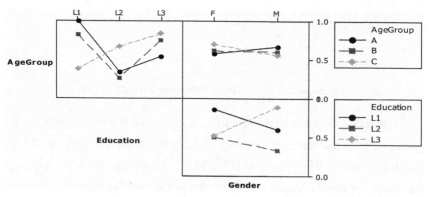

Figure 6.5.2　Interactions Plot upon Verbal Process

6.6 Impact of Age, Education and Gender on Behavioral Process Performance

The behavioral process is a type of transitivity that typically expresses human physiological and psychological behavior and that models the experiences like "smiling, dreaming, and staring." Of the 60 participants, each participant's overall behavioral process performances were identified by the two coders, and points were assigned to each participant. For example, the points of the 21st participant's behavioral process performances are 2.

Table 6.6.1 shows the details of how the 21st participant used the behavioral process and how the two coders identified the process. The verbs, 看**(look),** 躺**(lie),** were used by the 21st participant.

Table 6.6.1 The 21st Participant's Behavioral Process Performance

标号：_____

NO: 21

请仔细阅读每一段叙述，并在下面标出你能在每一段叙述中找到的粗体动词。要求叙述中的动词出现的环境与下面相同或相近。

Please read each narrative carefully, and mark out the following blackened verbs which you could find in each narrative. The verbs appear in the narrative should be the same as or similar to they appear in the following context.

5. 一个男孩(一个男人)在**看**。 (4)

    A boy (a man) **looks** on.

14. 男孩(那个男的/那个男的/那个男人)**躺**在掉下来的鸟巢附近， (4)

    While the boy (the male/ the man/ that man) **lies** near the fallen nest,

As for the participants' behavioral process performance in transitivity, age has a significant impact among the three age groups (50-59, 60-69 and 70-79). P is equal to 0.022 which is smaller than P = 0.05; thus, a statistically significant difference exists in the participants' behavioral process performances among the three age groups. See Table 6.6.2. This result is also contradictory to the results of Juncos-Rabadán, Pereiro and Rodríguez (2005) who reported that aging reduces density of informational content because the performances between Age Group 50-59 and Age Group 70-79 in the present research are similar.

Table 6.6.2   General Linear Model: Behavioral Process versus Age Group, Education, Gender

Factor	Type	Levels	Values
Age Group	fixed	3	A, B, C
Education	fixed	3	L1, L2, L3
Gender	fixed	2	F, M

Analysis of Variance for Behavioral Process, Using Adjusted SS for Tests

Source	DF	Seq SS	Adj SS	Adj MS	F	P
Age Group	2	2.2333	4.4878	2.2439	4.19	0.022
Education	2	0.2026	0.5626	0.2813	0.53	0.595
Gender	1	0.6550	0.3515	0.3515	0.66	0.423
Age Group*Education	4	4.4992	5.2825	1.3206	2.47	0.060
Age Group*Gender	2	0.8827	0.6099	0.3049	0.57	0.570
Education*Gender	2	0.2855	0.5763	0.2882	0.54	0.588
Age Group*Education*Gender	4	2.6750	2.6750	0.6688	1.25	0.305
Error	42	22.5000	22.5000	0.5357		
Total	59	33.9333				

DF: Degree of Freedom; Seq SS: Sequential Sums of Squares; Adj SS: Adjusted Sums of Squares; Adj MS: Adjusted Mean of Squares; F: Adj MS due to factor/Adj MS due to error; P: P-value

The present research shows that the trend of the three groups' behavioral process performances coincides with the participants' overall performances in the transitivity as a whole: The behavioral process performance of Age Group 60-69 is better than that of Age Group 50-59 and Age Group 70-79, and the behavioral process performance of Age Group 50-59 is similar to the performance of Age Group 70-79. Among the three age groups, the performance behavioral process of Age Group 60-69 is the highest. See Figure 6.6.1.

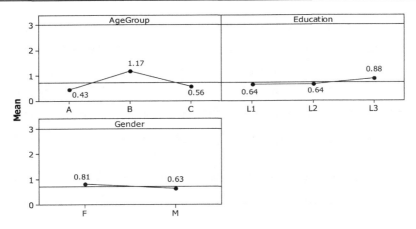

Figure 6.6.1   Main Effects Plot upon Behavioral Process

Education does not have a significant impact on the participants' behavioral process performances among the three age groups (50-59, 60-69 and 70-79). P is equal to 0.595, which is larger than P = 0.05. See Table 6.6.2.

Gender does not have a significant impact on the participants' behavioral process performance in transitivity among the three age groups (50-59, 60-69 and 70-79). P is equal to 0.423, which is larger than P = 0.05. See Table 6.6.2.

The main effects plot of age group, education and gender upon the participants' behavioral process performance appears visually in Figure 6.6.1. The effects of age group upon the participants' overall behavioral process performances in transitivity are larger compared to the effects of education and gender. The effects of gender upon the participants' overall behavioral process performances in transitivity are larger compared to the effects of education. Age group significantly affects the participants' overall behavioral process performances in transitivity. Education and gender do not have a statistically significant effect on the participants' overall behavioral process performances in transitivity.

As for the interactions among age, education and gender, the smallest P-value, 0.060 (see Table 6.6.2), appears in the interaction pair of age and education. This value is larger than P=0.05. Thus, the interactions of age and education do not have a significant impact on the participants' behavioral process performances in transitivity. The interactions of other pairs (age and gender with P=0.570, education and gender with P=0.588) do not have a significant impact on the participants' behavioral process performances in transitivity. The interactions of age, education and gender, as a whole, do not, statistically, have a significant impact on the participants' behavioral process performances in transitivity (P= 0.305). They do not make a statistically significant contribution to the effect on the participants' overall behavioral process performances in transitivity.

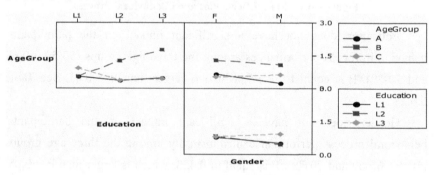

Figure 6.6.2   Interactions Plot upon Behavioral Process

6.7 Impact of Age, Education and Gender on Relational Process

The relational process is a main process of transitivity that typically expresses "being" behavior and that models relationships like "Tom is the boss; John has a book." Of the 60 participants, each participant's overall relational process performances were identified by the two coders. For example, the point of the 11th participant's relational process performance is 1. Table 6.7.1 shows the details of how the 11th participant used relational process and how the two coders identified it. The verb, 是 (be), was used by the 11th participant.

Table 6.7.1   The 11th Participant's Performance on Relational Process

标号：＿＿＿＿＿＿＿

NO:　　＿＿11＿＿

请仔细阅读每一段叙述，并在下面标出你能在每一段叙述中找到的粗体动词。要求叙述中的动词出现的环境与下面相同或相近。

Please read each narrative carefully, and mark out the following blackened verbs which you could find in each narrative. The verbs appear in the narrative should be the same as or similar to they appear in the following context.

2. 他们**是**一对恋人（一个男孩和一个女孩/一对夫妻/恋人/儿子和母亲）。　　(5)

　　They **are** lovers friends (a boy and a girl / husband and wife / lovers / son and mom).

In terms of the participants' overall relational process performances in transitivity, age does not have a significant impact among the three age groups (50-59, 60-69 and 70-79). P is equal to 0.252, which is larger than P = 0.05. No statistical difference exists in the participants' overall relational process performances among the three age groups. See Table 6.7.2. This is contradictory to the results of Juncos-Rabadán, Pereiro and Rodríguez (2005) who reported that age reduces density of informational content. Although a very small trend occurs which coincides with the participants' overall performances in the transitivity as a whole: the relational process performance of Age Group 60-69 is better than that of Age Group 50-59 and Age Group 70-79, and the relational process performance of Age Group 50-59 is similar to the performance of Age Group 70-79, these differences are too small to be considered because of the P-value.

Table 6.7.2   General Linear Model: Relational Process versus Age Group, Education, Gender

Factor	Type	Levels	Values
Age Group	fixed	3	A, B, C
Education	fixed	3	L1, L2, L3
Gender	fixed	2	F, M

Analysis of Variance for Relational Process, Using Adjusted SS for Tests

Source	DF	Seq SS	Adj SS	Adj MS	F	P
Age Group	2	1.0333	0.4148	0.2074	1.42	0.252
Education	2	0.1899	0.1899	0.0949	0.65	0.526
Gender	1	0.0014	0.0000	0.0000	0.00	0.987
Age Group*Education	4	0.5111	0.4258	0.1064	0.73	0.576
Age Group*Gender	2	0.1209	0.0519	0.0259	0.18	0.837
Education*Gender	2	0.1113	0.0555	0.0278	0.19	0.827
Age Group*Education*Gender	4	0.2487	0.2487	0.0622	0.43	0.788
Error	42	6.1167	6.1167	0.1456		
Total	59	8.3333				

DF: Degree of Freedom; Seq SS: Sequential Sums of Squares; Adj SS: Adjusted Sums of Squares; Adj MS: Adjusted Mean of Squares; F: Adj MS due to factor/Adj MS due to error; P: P-value

Education does not have a significant impact on the participants' relational process performances among the three age groups (50-59, 60-69 and 70-79). P is equal to 0.526, which is larger than P = 0.05. See Table 6.7.2.

Gender does not have a significant impact on the participants' overall relational process performances among the three age groups (50-59, 60-69 and 70-79). P is equal to 0.987, which is larger than P = 0.05. See Table 6.7.2.

The main effects plot of age group, education and gender upon the participants' relational process performance appears in Figure 6.7.1. The effects of age and education upon the participants' overall relational process performances in transitivity are larger compared to the effects of gender. However, all of them do not statistically affect the participants' overall relational process performances in transitivity.

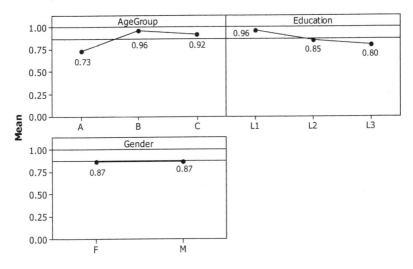

Figure 6.7.1   Main Effects Plot upon Relational Process

As for the interactions among age, education and gender, the smallest P-value appears in the interaction pair of age and education in which the P-value is 0.576. This value is larger than P=0.05. Thus, the interaction of age and education does not have a significant impact on the participants' relational process performances in transitivity. The interactions of other pairs (age and gender with P=0.837, education and gender with P = 0.827) do not have a significant impact on the participants' relational process performances in transitivity; the interactions of age, education and gender, as a whole, do not have a statistically significant impact on the participants' relational process performances in transitivity (P = 0.788). They do not make a statistically significant contribution to the effect on the participants' overall relational process performances in transitivity.

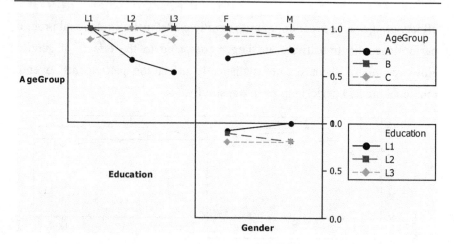

Figure 6.7.2   Interactions Plot upon Relational Process

The study of relational process finds that "be" may not be necessary in relational process in Chinese. For example, in"他在医院里。(He in hospital)", there is no "be". Thus, "be" is unnecessary in Chinese. Thus, the meaning of the verb "be" in relational process can be implied in Chinese rather than the necessity of being present in English.

6.8 Impact of Age, Education and Gender on Existential Process Performance

The existential process is a type of transitivity that typically expresses "existing" and that models the experiences like "There are two chairs in the room." Of the 60 participants, each participant's overall existential process performance was identified by the two coders. For example, the point of the 14th participant's existential process performance is 1. Table 6.8.1 shows the details of how the 14th participant used the existential process and how the two coders identified it. The verb, 是 (are), was used by the 14th participant.

Table 6.8.1   The 14ᵗʰ Participant's Performance on Existential Process

标号：_____

NO: ___14___

请仔细阅读每一段叙述，并在下面标出你能在每一段叙述中找到的粗体动词。要求叙述中的动词出现的环境与下面相同或相近。

Please read each narrative carefully, and mark out the following blackened verbs which you could find in each narrative. The verbs appear in the narrative should be the same as or similar to they appear in the following context.

1. 图中有两个人（一个男人和一个女人/一个男孩和一个女孩/一对夫妻/一对恋人）。   (6**)

   There **are** two persons (a man and a woman / a boy and a girl / husband and wife/ lovers) in the picture.

The present research results show that age does not have a significant impact on the participants' overall existential process performances in transitivity among the three age groups (50-59, 60-69 and 70-79). P is equal to 0.511, which is larger than P = 0.05. Thus, no statistically significant difference exists in the participants' overall existential process performances among the three age groups. See Table 6.8.2.

Education does not have a significant impact on the participants' overall existential process performance among the three age groups (50-59, 60-69 and 70-79). P is equal to 0.373, which is larger than P = 0.05. See Table 6.8.2.

Gender does not have a significant impact on the participants' overall existential process performances in transitivity among the three age groups (50-59, 60-69 and 70-79). P is equal to 0.680, which is larger than P = 0.05. See Table 6.8.2.

Table 6.8.2　General Linear Model: Existential Process versus Age Group, Education, Gender

Factor	Type	Levels	Values
Age Group	fixed	3	A, B, C
Education	fixed	3	L1, L2, L3
Gender	fixed	2	F, M

Analysis of Variance for Existential Process, Using Adjusted SS for Tests

Source	DF	Seq SS	Adj SS	Adj MS	F	P
Age roup	2	0.4000	0.3019	0.1509	0.68	0.511
Education	2	0.3653	0.4464	0.2232	1.01	0.373
Gender	1	0.1041	0.0382	0.0382	0.17	0.680
Age Group*Education	4	1.0888	1.0563	0.2641	1.19	0.327
Age Group*Gender	2	0.6067	0.7073	0.3536	1.60	0.214
Education*Gender	2	0.7019	0.5613	0.2807	1.27	0.291
Age Group*Education*Gender	4	1.0998	1.0998	0.2750	1.24	0.307
Error	42	9.2833	9.2833	0.2210		
Total	59	13.6500				

DF: Degree of Freedom; Seq SS: Sequential Sums of Squares; Adj SS: Adjusted Sums of Squares; Adj MS: Adjusted Mean of Squares; F: Adj MS due to factor / Adj MS due to error; P: P-value

The present research results are contradictory to the results of Juncos-Rabadán, Pereiro and Rodríguez (2005) who reported that aging reduces density of informational content for the reason that Age Group 50-59 and Age Group 60-69 performed very similarly in existential process in transitivity. See Figure 6.8.1.

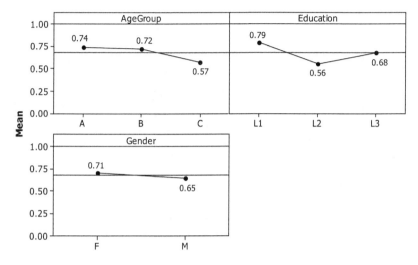

Figure 6.8.1   Main Effects Plot upon Existential Process

As for the interactions among age, education and gender, the P- value that appears in the interaction pair of age and education is 0.327. See Table 6.8.2. It is large (larger than 0.05 significance level) enough to say that no interaction exists between age and education. Thus, the interaction of age and education does not have a significant impact on the participants' existential process performance in transitivity. For the same reason, the interactions of other pairs (age and gender with $p = 0.214$, education and gender with $p = 0.291$) do not have a significant impact on the participants' existential process performances in transitivity; the interactions of age, education and gender, as a whole, do not, statistically, have a significant impact on the participants' existential process performances ($P = 0.788$). They do not have a significant contribution to an effect on the participants' overall existential process performances in transitivity. See Table 6.8.2 and Figure 6.8.2.

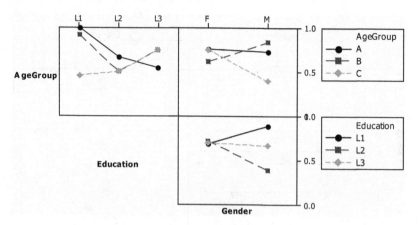

Figure 6.8.2   Interactions Plot upon Existential Process

6.9 Summary of Age, Education and Gender Impact on Transitivity

The six processes in transitivity provide a more detailed understanding of how participants' experiences and responses are construed than the traditional simple bi-division of verbs as transitive and intransitive verbs. The participants' experiences of "doing, sensing, being, etc." are clearly revealed in the narratives, and allow analysis. Table 6.9.1 shows that more aspects of verbs are revealed in terms of transitivity than considering traditional transitive and intransitive verbs.

Table 6.9.1   Comparison of Transitivity and Traditional Bi-Division

Transitivity	Definition	Traditional Verb Functions	Object
Material	Processes of "doing"	Transitive	+
		Intransitive	−
Relational	Processes of "being", "having", and "being"	Transitive	+
		Intransitive	−
Mental	Processes of sensing: feeling, thinking, and perceiving	Transitive	+
		Intransitive	−

Continued

Transitivity	Definition	Traditional Verb Functions	Object
Verbal	Processes of "saying"	Transitive	+
		Intransitive	−
Behavioral	Physiological/Psychological process	Transitive	+
		Intransitive	−
Existential	Processes of existing	Intransitive	−

The final part of this chapter, for sake of convenience and clarity, summarizes the results of age, education and gender effects on the participants' performance in transitivity and its sub-categories.

1. The results indicate that age can have a significant impact on the participants' overall performance in transitivity among the three age groups (50-59, 60-69 and 70-79). (See Table 6.9.2.)

2. The present study shows that the points of participants' performances increase from Age Group 50-59 to Age Group 60-69, and the points of participants' performances decrease from Age Group 60-69 to Age Group 70-79. The tendency of the age group's performances in transitivity is like a "∧" shape that appears in Figure 6.2.1. The performances of Age Group 60-69 in transitivity are better than those of Age Group 50-59 and Age Group 70-79 respectively. The performances of Age Group 60-69 in transitivity are the highest among the three age groups. The performances of Age Group 50-59 are similar to Age Group 70-79 in transitivity, or the performances of Age Group 70-79 are at least not lower than the performances of Age Group 50-59 in transitivity. See Table 6.2.2 and Figure 6.2.1.

3. The present research shows that age has a significant impact on the participants' behavioral process performances in transitivity among the three age groups (50-59, 60-69 and 70-79). The trend of three groups' performances coincides with the participants' performances in transitivity as a whole: The performances of Age Group 60-69 in transitivity are better than those of Age Group 50-59 and Age Group

70-79; the performances of Age Group 50-59 in transitivity are similar to Age Group 70-79, and among the three age groups, the behavioral process performances of Age Group 60-69 in transitivity are the highest. See Table 6.6.2 and Figure 6.6.1.

4. The present research shows that age does not have a significant impact on the participants' material, mental, verbal relational and existential process performances in transitivity among the three age groups (50-59, 60-69 and 70-79). However, although the impact is insignificant, the trend of three age groups' performances in the material, mental and relational processes is in agreement with the participants' overall performances in overall transitivity: The performance of Age Group 60-69 is better than that of Age Group 50-59 and Age Group 70-79, and the performance of Age Group 50-59 is similar to Age Group 70-79. Among the three age groups, the performance of Age Group 60-69 in transitivity is the highest.

5. The present research does not find any interactions in any two-factor groups; it also does not find any statistically significant interactions in the three-factor group.

6. Verb "be" may be unnecessary in relational process in Mandarin Chinese as shown in section 6.7.

Table 6.9.2   Significant Impact of Age, Education and Gender

	Factor(s) Groups	Significance		
Overall Transitivity	Age Group	Yes		
	Education	No		
	Gender	No		
	Age vs. Education	No		
	Age vs. Gender	No		
	Education vs. Gender	No		
	Age vs. Education vs. Gender	No		
Material	Age Group	No		
	Education	No		
	Gender	No		

Continued

	Factor(s) Groups	Significance		
Material	Age vs. Education	No		
	Age vs. Gender	No		
	Education vs. Gender	No		
	Age vs. Education vs. Gender	No		
Relational	Age Group	No		
	Education	No		
	Gender	No		
	Age vs. Education	No		
	Age vs. Gender	No		
	Education vs. Gender	No		
	Age vs. Education vs. Gender	No		
Mental	Age Group	No		
	Education	No		
	Gender	No		
	Age vs. Education	No		
	Age vs. Gender	No		
	Education vs. Gender	No		
	Age vs. Education vs. Gender	No		
Verbal	Age Group	No		
	Education	No		
	Gender	No		
	Age vs. Education	No		
	Age vs. Gender	No		
	Education vs. Gender	No		
	Age vs. Education vs. Gender	No		
Behavioral	Age Group	Yes		
	Education	No		
	Gender	No		
	Age vs. Education	No		
	Age vs. Gender	No		
	Education vs. Gender	No		
	Age vs. Education vs. Gender	No		
Existential	Age Group	No		
	Education	No		
	Gender	No		

Continued

	Factor(s) Groups	Significance		
Existential	Age vs. Education	No		
	Age vs. Gender	No		
	Education vs. Gender	No		
	Age vs. Education vs. Gender	No		

Chapter 7   CONCLUSION

Chapter 7, the final chapter of the dissertation, briefly reiterates the objectives of the present research, concisely summarizes the findings of the present research and explains the analysis process. After discussing and defending the strengths of the present research, this chapter critically evaluates the present research by identifying its limitations and suggests directions for future research.

7.1 Summary of the Objectives, Results and Analysis

As mentioned early in the introduction (see Chapter 1), the present research consists of four objectives: 1) to revise and modify the too generalized results of age impact on language as reported by the previous researchers; 2) to gain a new and detailed understanding of age, education and gender impact on Chinese elders' performance in transitivity; 3) to experimentally and statistically test the assumption of Makoni, Lin and Schrauf (2005) who predicted that education cannot affect the elders' performance in picture elicited narratives; and 4) to explore the insights gained regarding the impact of Chinese aging in using transitivity, and the contribution these insights make to the understanding of transitivity.

The results of the present study show that transitivity and its sub-categories can reveal more comprehensive and more detailed information about the participants than the traditional approach of the division of transitive and intransitive in terms of objects. The results also indicate that age, statistically, can have a significant impact on the participants' performance in transitivity, and the relationship between the participants' age and their performance is not a straight line simply describing the increase or decrease of those performance as the participants' age increases. Rather, the graphic representation assumes a "∧" shape: the points of the participants' performance in transitivity show an increase from Age Group 50-59 to Age Group 60-69, while the points of participants' performance show a decrease from Age Group 60-69 to Age Group 70-79. Also, Age Group 50-59 and Age Group 70-79 perform in a very similar way in transitivity. Education and gender do not statistically have a significant impact on the participants' overall transitivity performance among the three age groups (50-59, 60-69 and 70-79 years old). The present research does not find any statistically significant interactions in any two-factor groups; nor does it find it also does not find statistically significant interactions in the three-factor groups. The results indicate that the verb "to be" is unnecessary in the relational process in Chinese, and this can be a contribution to SFT when considering the linguistic characteristics of Chinese.

The analysis of the data has been accomplished in terms of transitivity and GLM (General Linear Model). In order to explore the objectives, the present research used transitivity in SFT as a theoretical framework; the two raters encoded the participants' data according the standard of the coding system (see Chapter 5), and transitivity and the sub-categories of the transitivity were labeled on the coding sheets (see Appendix A). In order to determine the impact of age, education and gender on the participants' performance in the use of transitivity and the subcategories of transitivity, GLM in ANOVA was the method used to analyze the encoded data. The reason for using GLM is that not only the factors (age, education and gender) and the levels (three age groups, three education level groups and two gender groups) but also the interactions of the factors and the levels are taken into account. The impact of age, education and gender is found by statistical calculation.

7.2 Strengths of the Present Research

This section briefly discusses and defends the strengths of the present research, which focuses on transitivity, development of coding system and the proper use of GLM.

7.2.1 Transitivity as a Proper Framework for an Aging Study

One strength of the present research is the use of transitivity in SFT as a theoretical framework since transitivity provides a solution to the problem confronted by Makoni, Lin and Schrauf (2005). As mentioned in Chapter 1, Makoni, Lin and Schrauf accurately reported the problem of their research: "The analysis is complicated because it is difficult to use Western views when analyzing Chinese texts" (Makoni, et al, 2005, p117). Transitivity has taken Chinese philosophy into account; it contains the idea of Yin and Yang, and it also is compatible with Chinese philosophy, as demonstrated in detail in Chapter 3. Thus, transitivity can provide a solution to Makoni, Lin and Schrauf's problem.

The results of the present study show that transitivity and its sub-categories can reveal more comprehensive and more detailed information about the participants' performance than the traditional approach of the transitive and intransitive division in relation to objects. The present research found how the participants performed, not only in transitivity as a whole, but also in each of the material, mental, verbal, behavioral, relational and existential process. In contrast, if the traditional approach of transitive verbs and intransitive verbs is used, the only revelation would be whether or not a verb needs an object, and it would be impossible to systematically explain the verb in terms of meaning or experience. For details, see Chapter 6.

7.2.2 Justification of Paradis' Stimuli and Development of Coding System

The second strength of the present research is the justification of Paradis' stimuli and the development of a coding system. No requirements exist for the relational and existential processes in the stimuli of Paradis (1987), so the experience of existence and relation was absent, and the participants' performances in relational and existential processes, important experience, were neglected. When applying a transitivity system to the development of coding system and data analysis in this study, and relational and existential processes become constituents of the coding system, more details of the participants' performance become apparent. Adding and using relational and existential processes to guide data analysis are a contribution of the present research. And the importance of relational and existential processes in Chinese is recognized.

The relational process is significantly important and pervasive in Chinese daily life. Chinese people like to talk, ask or guess the relationships among people, especially when a Chinese encounter two people of different genders. Which is different from that in the Western world where the relationship between two people of different genders is considered as a private matter? Attempts to discern the relationships among people may provide a clue for Chinese to understand the roles of people whom they meet or see, and this can provide useful information for providing the impetus for the observer to react in a proper way.

The existential process is also very important in Chinese participants' narratives. It expresses the existence of people or things in a specific environment or location. The existential process shows a person's (participant's) general understanding of a story. The present research shows that 40 participants of the total 60 used the existential process in their narratives. This indicates that Chinese participants tend to know the background or settings in which people or things are situated.

7.2.3 Proper Use of GLM to Determine Significant Impact

The third strength of present research is the use of GLM in ANOVA that analyze those data and find the results to prove Hypotheses 2 to 4 (Chapter 4). When using GLM, not only the factors and the levels but also the interactions of the factors and the levels are considered. Thus, the impact of age, education and gender can be found by statistical calculation. The results in Chapter 6 prove the validity of Hypotheses 2 to 4 (For details, see Chapter 6).

7.3 Limitations

"Every coin has two sides." This section critically evaluates the other side of the coin—the limitations of the present research.

7.3.1 Absence of Post-Reflective Comment

The first limitation of the present research is the absence of post-reflective comment, which means the absence of allowing participants to make their comments on their narratives elicited from the pictures of The Bird Nest Story. Thus, what the participants feel and think about their narratives remains unknown. Knowing the participants' feelings and comments regarding themselves and about the pictures might be interesting, but that knowledge would require considerable time and effort to record post-reflective comments from 60 participants. However, since the purpose of the present research is to compare these results with those of the previous researches and to revise the conclusions of previous researchers, the absence of post-reflective comments has no influence on the results of the present study.

7.3.2 Quasi-Longitudinal Study and No True Longitudinal Study

The second limitation of the current research is the data collection from the quasi-longitudinal age groups, which refer to collecting data from different age groups simultaneously. That is, the present research uses different age groups at one particular time, and these groups coexist at the same time, when in fact they are not of the same groups across different decades. In this sense, they are quasi-longitudinal. The remaining question is whether or not the study of longitudinal age groups is possible. The answer depends on whether or not the research can follow the age groups across different time periods. Since the true age group changes from time to time, following the entire age group over a long period without losing track of them would be extremely difficult and time consuming. The likelihood of a researcher following a group for twenty, thirty or even forty years to complete the research is small, indeed. For example, if the difference between the two contingent age groups is ten years old in the data of the present research, ten years are necessary for people of one age group to transit to the next age group, creating great difficulty for a graduate school researcher to maintain observations and identify changes over the intervening decade.

7.3.3 No Requirement for Processing Speed

The third limitation is that the present research does not set a requirement for processing speed, which is very important to some psychologists. Processing speed refers to how quickly a person can proceed or react, and some in American post-war psychology considered it related to intelligence. The more quickly a person reacts, apparently, the smarter that person is. In this sense, processing speed of elderly people can reveal their mental status to a certain extent. However, a different psychology exists in which slow reaction may imply wisdom (Danziger, 1997). The slow reaction may suggest that an elderly person wants to think carefully, proceed cautiously, thus providing an effective solution for the required task. For this reason, the present study does not set a requirement for processing speed. A participant's completion of a narrative within certain amount of time is acceptable. This may be a more realistic rather than limiting aspect since elders usually have more time to complete their tasks in real life, and no one would constrain them to a time limit.

7.4 Recommendations for Future Research

7.4.1 Extension of Age-Span

The extension of age-span can provide a fuller aging picture. The present research investigated the impact of age, education and gender on the participants' performances in transitivity among the age groups of 50-59, 60-69 and 70-79; however, the question of how the other age groups beyond these age groups (for example, the age group of 80-89) can perform in transitivity remains unknown. In order to have a better understanding of aging in terms of age-span, the recommendation is to recruit participants who belong to the age group of 80-89, or even the age group of 90-100. These age groups involve declining performance in transitivity. But difficulty remains for recruiting participants for these age groups because the number of people who fit the criteria is few in comparison to other age groups due to the Chinese average life expectancy (around 70). Another concern is whether or not the elders in age groups of 80-89 are 90-100 are willing to attend to the research since they need to prove that they have no history of neurological or psychiatric illness, or other problems that might directly influence the performance of telling a story. This means that extending participation to these additional age groups is particularly more complicated than simply looking at the pictures and telling a Bird Nest Story.

7.4.2 The Comparison of Normal Elders with Elderly Patients

A comparison of normal elders with elderly patients will be beneficial. The present research examined the impact of age, education and gender on the normal elderly participants' performances in transitivity. As mentioned early, the normal participants refer to those who had no history of neurological or psychiatric illness, or other problems that might directly influence the performance of telling a story. However, some elderly people suffer from neurological or psychiatric illness or have a history of neurological or psychiatric illness, and how these patients can perform in transitivity remains unclear. An interesting and useful investigation would be to compare normal elders and elderly patients of the same age groups to find their performance differences in transitivity. Certain neurological or psychiatric illnesses may relate to certain misuse or missing transitivity or certain types of processes inside transitivity; the result of future research can provide a guide or help to medical professionals for diagnosing their patients. So a comparison between the normal elders and elderly patients of the same age groups is recommended for future research.

7.4.3 Mini-Lingual Status Examination

Development of a mini-lingual status examination would be useful for future research. Mini-lingual status examination is a concept created by the current study's researcher by imitating the word formation of the "mini-mental status examination" used in testing for Alzheimer's disease. Mini-lingual status examination reveals the lowest level that a normal elder can perform in transitivity and in certain processes inside transitivity, namely the language level that a normal elder can reach easily irrelevant of gender and education. Once the mini-lingual examination is established for the normal elders, the missing or abnormal use of some of the items or the combination of the items in the mini-lingual examination might imply that something might be wrong with the elder, and then a further diagnosis for this elder might be needed. However, research of this type would be very difficult because it will need the cooperation of researchers, medical professionals, patients and patients' guardians.

7.4.4 Semi-Computerized Coding

Coding is a necessary yet very time consuming procedure in the present research. The two raters manually coded all the data, and required significant energy. Toward the end stage of the research, the author found the labor intensity required for coding the data can be reduced to some extent with the assistance of computer coding. Computers can identify the verbs required in the coding sheet, and label them. Then the raters can concentrate on the labeled verbs and look at the environment in which the labeled verbs appear. This method can reduce coding labor intensity and improve accuracy.

7.5 Final Remarks

Age impact on transitivity is very complicated, and one needs to be very cautious when discussing declining or decreasing content in narrative language of the elderly as they age. The present research results show the participants' performances increase from Age Group 50-59 to Age Group 60-69, and the present research results also show that the participants' performances decrease from Age Group 60-69 to Age Group 70-79.

Transitivity declines when one becomes older. However, necessary clarifications are whether or not declination in transitivity can contribute to a statistically significant change from one age group to another, and how the changes tend to be in a specific language in terms of increase or decrease. Asserting that language would decline as one ages without specifying age groups or native languages is, in itself, inaccurate.

REFERENCES

Armstrong, E. (2002) "Variation in the Discourse of Non-Brain Damaged Speakers on a Clinical Task." *Aphasiology,* 16: 647-658.

Armstrong, E. (2002) "A Review of Constructing (In)Competence". *International Journal of Language and Communication Discourse* , 37(1).

Armstrong, E. (2005) Expressing Opinions and Feelings in Aphasia: Linguistic Options. *Aphasiology,* 19 (3/4/5): 285-295.

Berko (Gleason), J. (1958) The Child's Learning of English Morphology. *Word,* 14, 150-177.

Berko Gleason, J., Goodglass, H., Ackerman, N., Green, E., & Hyde, M. R. (1975) Retrieval of Syntax in Broca's Aphasia. *Brain and Language,* 2, 451-471.

Berko Gleason, J., Goodglass, H., Obler, L., Green, E., Hyde, M. R., & Weintraub, S. (1980) "Narrative Strategies of Aphasic and Normal-speaking Subjects." *Journal of Speech and Hearing research,* 3, 257-267

Berstein, B. (1971) *Class, Codes and Control, Volume I: theoretical studies toward a sociology of language,* London: Routledge & Kegan Paul.

Bernstein, B. (1990) *The Structuring of Pedagogic Discourse, Volume IV: Class, Codes and Control.* London: Routledge

Berry, M. (1995) "Thematic Options and Success in Writing", in Buler, C. S., Cardwell R. A. and Channell J. (eds.) *Language and Literature –Theory and Practice: A Tribute to Walter Grauberg* (Univerisy of Nottingham Monographs in the Humanities VI) Nottingham: University of Nottingham, pp 62-80

Berry, M. (1996), What is Theme?-A(nother) Personal View, in Berry, M., Butler, C., Fawcett, R. and Huang, G. (eds.) Meaning and Form: Systemic Functional Interactions. *Advances in Discourse Processes*. Vol. LVII

Bloomfield, L. (1933) *Language*. New York Henry Holt.

Botvin, G. and Sutton-Smith, B. (1977) The Development of Structural Complexity in Children's Narratives. *Developmental Psychology* 13, (377-388)

Cheng, X. (2002) Two Problems about the Relational Processes in Transitivity. *Modern Foreign Languages (Quarterly)* Vol. 25 No. 3 311-317 (Chinese Journal)

Cohen, G. (1979). Language Comprehension in Old Age. *Cognitive Psychology,* 11, 412-429.

Chomsky, N. (1957) *Syntactic Structures*. The Hague: Mouton.

Chomsky, N. (1965) *Aspects of the Theory of Syntax*. Cambridge, Mass.: MIT Press.de Bot, K and Makoni S. (2005) *Language and Aging in Multilingual Contexts* by Multilingual Matter Ltd. Clevedon. Buffalo. Toronto

Danziger, K. (1997) *Naming the Mind, How psychology Found its Language.* SAGE Publications. London, Thousand Oaks, New Delhi

Ding, S. (2007) On the Foundation of the Description of the Semantic Compositional Scale in the Ideational Metafunction. *Foreign Languages and Their Teaching* (Chinese Journal)

Draper, N.R. and Smith, H. (1998), Applied Regression Analysis, Publisher: New York: John Wiley & Sons, 1998, 3rd edition

Fawcett, R. P. (1980). *Cognitive Linguistic and Social Interaction: Towards an Integrated Model of a Systemic Functional Grammar and the other Components of an Interacting Mind.* Heidelberg/Exeter: Julius Groos/Exeter University Press.

Fawcett, R. P. (1987). The Semantics of Clause and Verb of Relational Processes in English. In Halliday, M. A. K. & Fawcett, R. (eds.), *New*

Developments in Systemic Linguistics. Volume 1: Theory and Description. London: Frances Pinter. 130-183

Firth, J. R. (1957) *Papers on Linguistics* 1934-51. London: Oxford Giles, H., Coupland, N. and Coupland, J. (1992) Intergenerational Talk and Communication with Older People. *Journal of Aging and Human Development* 34 (4), 271-297

Goodglass, H.(2000) Jean Berko Gleason's Contribution to Aphasia Research: Pioneering Techniques. In Menn and Ratner (Eds) (2000) *Methods of Study in Language Production.* Mahwah, N J: Lawrence Erlbaum Associates, Inc.

Goodglass, H., & Kaplan, E. (1983). *The Assessment of Aphasia and Related Disorders.* Philadelphia: Lea & Febiger.

Goodglass, H., & Kaplan, E. (1983). *The Boston Diagnostic Aphasia Examination.* Philadelphia: Lea & Febiger.

Goodglass, H., Christiansen, J.A., & Gallagher, R. (1993) Comparison of Morphology and Syntax in Free Narrative and Structured Tests: Fluent vs Nonfluent Aphasics. *Cortex,* 29 (23), 377-407.

Gregory, M. (1967) Aspects of Varieties Differentiation. *Journal of Linguistics.* 3. 177-198.

Halliday, M. A. K., McIntosh, A. and Strevens, P. (1964) *The Linguistic Sciences and Language Teaching.* London: Longman.

Halliday, M. A. K. (1966). Notes on Transitivity and Theme in English. *Journal of Linguistics,* 2.1, 1966, pp. 57-67; 3.1, 1967, pp. 37-81; 3.2, 1967, pp. 199-244; 4.2, 1968, pp. 179-215.

Halliday, M. A. K. (1973). *Explorations in the Functions of Language.* London: Edward Arnold.

Halliday, M. A. K. (1975) *Learning How to Mean.* London: Edward Arnold.

Halliday, M. A. K. (1978) Language as Social Semiotic: The Social Interpretation of Language and Meaning. London: Edward Arnold.

Halliday, M.A. K., & Hasan, R. (1976). *Cohesion in English.* London: Longman

Halliday, M. A. K. (2000). *An Introduction to Functional Grammar.* Foreign Language Teaching and Research Press, Beijing, Edward Arnold Publishers.

Halliday M. A. K. & Fawcett, R. eds. (1987). *New Developments in Systemic Linguistics. Volume 1: Theory and Description.*

Halliday, M. A. K. (1985). *An Introduction to Functional Grammar* London: Edward Arnold.

Halliday, M. A. K. (2004). *An Introduction to Functional Grammar.* Edward Arnold Publishers.

Halliday, M.A. K. (2002) *Linguistic Studies of Text and Discourse* edited by Jonathan Webster. Continuum. London, New York

Halliday, M. A. K., & Matthiessen, C.M.I.M.(1999, 2000, 2001,2002). *Construing Experience Through Meaning: A Language Based Approach to Cognition.* London: Continuum.

Hasan, R. (2005) Semiotic mediation and three exotropic theories: Vygotsky, Halliday and Bernstein. In *Language Society and Consciousness.* The Collected Works of Ruqaiya Hasan, Vol. 1. London: Equinox.

Huang, G. (1996) eds. with Berry, M., Butler, C., and Fawcett R. Meaning and Form: Systemic Functional Interactions. *Advances in Discourse Processes.* Vol. LVII.

Huang, G. (2002) Hallidayan Linguistics in China. *World Englishes.* Vol. 21, No. 2 pp. 281-290, 2002

Hu, Z. L. (1994). *Discourse Cohesion and Coherence .* Shanghai Foreign Language Education Press. Shanghai, China

Isixsigma(2004), http://www.isixsigma.com/dictionary/Covariate-529. htm, Oct., 2004

Jackson, R., & Howe, N. (2004). *The Graying of the Middle Kingdom: The Demographics and Economics of Retirement Policy in China.* Washington, D.C.: Center for Strategic and International Studies.

Jesperson, O. (1965). *A Modern English Grammar on Historical Principles.* London: Allen &Unwin.

Jöreskog, K.G., & Sörbom, D. (1993). *LISREL 8: Structural Equation Modeling with the SIMPLIS Command Language*. Hillsdale, NJ: Erlbaum.

Kemper, S., Rash, S., Kynette, D. & Norman, J. (1990) Telling Stories: The Structure of Adults' Narratives. *European Journal of Cognitive Psychology* 2, 205-208

Levene, H. (1960). Contributions to Probability and Statistics, pp.278-292. Stanford University Press, CA.

Li, Chi, Zhang & Guo (2006). Comparison of health services use by Chinese urban and rural older adults in Yunnan province *Geriatr Gerontol Int* **6:** *260-269*

Lindsay, J., & Wilkinson, R. (1999). Repair Sequences in Aphasic Talk: A Comparison of Aphasic-Speech and Language Therapist and Aphasic-Spouse Conversations. Aphasiology, 13 (4/5), 305-326.

Makoni, S. (1997) Gerontolinguistics in South Africa, *International Journal of Applied Linguistics,* 7, 57-66

Makoni, S., &Makoe, P. (2001) Are African Susceptible to Dementia? Preliminary Reflections on Linguistic behavior in Aged Care and the Discourse in Xhosa of a Dementing White Bilingual. In E. Ridge, S. Makoni, & S. Ridge (Eds), *Freedom and discipline: Essays in Applied Linguistics from Southern Africa* (pp. 149-170). India: Bahri Publisher.

Makoni, S., Ridge, E., & Ridge, S. (2000) Through Different Lenses: An Analysis of the Writing History of a Dementia Person over Fifty Years. *Southern African   Journal of Applied Language Studies,* 19, 35-50.

Makoni, S., Grainger, K. (2002) Comparative Genrontolinguistics: Characterizing Discourses in Caring Institutions in South Africa and the United Kingdom. *Journal of Social Issues*, Vol. 58, No. 4 pp. 805-824

Makoni, S., Lin, W., & Schrauf, R. (2005) Effects of Age and Education in Older Chinese in the USA, *Language and Aging in Multilingual Contexts* by Kees de Bot and Sinfree Makoni. Multilingual Matter Ltd. Clevedon. Buffalo. Toronto

Martin, J. R. & Rothery, J. (1980), *Writing Project: Report 1980: Working Papers in Linguistics* 1. Department of Linguistics, University of Sydney.

Martin, J. R. & Rothery, J. (1986), "What a Functional Approach to the Writing Task Can Show Teachers about Good Writing" in Couture, B. (ed.) *Functional Approaches to Writing: Research Perspectives.* Norwook, N.J. : Ablex.

Martin, J. R. (1992), English Text: System and Structure. Amsterdam and Philadelphia: Benjamins.

Melrose, R. (2005), How a Neurological Account of Language can be Reconciled with a Linguist's Account of Language: The case of systemic-functional linguistics. *Journal of Neurolinguistics.* Volume 18, Issue 5 , September, Pages 401-421

Menn, L., and Ratner, N. (Eds) (2000) *Methods of Studying Language Production.* Mahwah, N J: Lawrence Erlbaum Associates, Inc.

Minitab Inc. (2000),   *Minitab 13*, help, 2000, Minitab Inc.

Montgomery, Douglas C (2002), *Design and analysis of experiments*, New York: John Wiley 2001, 5th Edition

Morton, D., Stanford, E., Happersett, C. and Mogaad, C. (1992) Acculturation and Functional Impairment Among older Chinese and Vietnamese in San Diego County. *Journal of Cross-cultural Gerontology* 7, 151-76

Noels, K., Cai, D., Turray, D. and Giles, L. (1999). Perceptions of Intergenerational and Intragenerational Communication in the United States of America and the People's Republic of China. *South Pacific Journal of Psychology* 10, 120-35.

Onésimo Juncos-Rabadán (1994). The Assessment of Bilingual in Normal Aging with the Bilingual Aphasia Test. *Journal of Neurolinguistics*

Onésimo Juncos-Rabadán (1996). Narrative Speech in the Elderly: Effects of Age and Education on Telling Stories. *International Journal of Behavioral Development*

Onésimo Juncos-Rabadán, Arturo X. Pereiro, María Soledad Rodríguez (2005). Narrative speech in aging: Quantity, information content, and cohesion. *Brain and Language.*

Pan (2003) Expressivities of Transitivity Analysis in Describing Stylistic Features. *Shandong Foreign Language Teaching.* Vol. 4 19- 23. (Chinese Journal)

Paradis, M. (2004). *A Neurolinguistic Theory of Bilingualism.* Amsterdam/ Philadelphia: John Benjamin's.

Paradis, M. (1987) *The Assessment of Bilingual Aphasia.* Lawrence Erlbaum Associates, Publishers. Hillsdale, New Jersey

Pereiro Rozas A. X.; Juncos Rabadan O. (2000). Referencia cohesiva no discurso narrativo na vellez (Cohesive reference of narrative discourse in elderly) (La référence cohésive dans le discours narratif des personnes âgées) *Verba (Verba)* ISSN 0210-377X vol. 27, pp. 317-339 (3 p.1/2)

Pfeiffer, E. (1975) A Short Portable Mental Status Questionnaire for the Assessment of Organic Brain Deficit in Elderly Patients. *Journal of the American Geriatrics Society* 10, 433-441

Prideaux, G. (1985). *Psycholinguistics: The Experimental Study of Language.* New York: Guilford Press.

Quirk, R. et al. (1985) *A Comprehensive Grammar of the English Language.* London: Longman.

Ratner, N., and Menn, L. (2000) In the Beginning was the Wug: Forty Years of Language Elicitation in (Eds) (2000) *Methods of Studying Language Production.* Mahwah, N J: Lawrence Erlbaum Associates, Inc.

Rubin, K. (1974). The relationship between spatial and communicative egocentrism in children and young and old adults. *Journal of Genetic Psychology,* 125, 295-301.

Triola, Mario F.(2000), Elementary Statistics, Publisher: Addison Wesley Longman, Inc., 8th ed.

Ulatowska, H.K., Allard, L., Reyes, B.A., Ford, J., & Chapman, S. (1992).

Conversational Discourse in Aphasia. *Aphasiology*, 6, 325-331

United Nations (2005). *World Population Prospects the 2004 Revision: Population Database.* New York: Department of Economic and Social Affairs, Population Division, United Nations Population Division.

Waldman, C. (2005) China's Demographic Destiny and Its Economic Implications. *Business Economics.* Oct. 2005; 40, 4; ABI/INFORM Global, 32-45

Wang, W., Wu, S., Cheng, X., Dai, H., Ross, K., Du, X, Yin, W., (2000), Prevalence of Alzheimer's Disease and Other Dementing Disorders in a Urban Community of Beijing, China. *Neuroepidemiology* 19, 194-200

Wells, G. (1999), *Dialogic Inquiry: Towards a Sociocultural Practice and Theory of Education.* Cambridge University Press

Wodak, R. (1981) Women relate, men report. *Journal of Pragmatics 5. 261-85*

Wodak, R. (1986) *Language Behavior in Therapy Groups.* Los Angles: University of California Press

Woo, J., Ho, S., Yuen, Y., Yu, L. and Lau, J. (1996). An Estimation of Functional Disability in Elderly Chinese Aged 70 and Over. *Disability and Rehabilitation* 18 (12), 609-612

World Population: http://esa.un.org/unpp/p2k0data.asp

Yin, B., & Yao, R. (2006) Consumption Patterns of Chinese Elders: Evidence from A Survey in Wuhan, China. J Fam Econ Iss (2006) 27: 702-714 Published online: 13 September 2006 _ Springer Science+Business Media, Inc. 2006

Zeng, Y. and Vaupel, J. (2002). Functional Capacity and Self Evaluation of Health and Life of Oldest Old in China. *Journal of Social Issues: International Perspectives on the Well-being of Older Adults.* 58 (4), 733-49

Zhu, Y. S., Zheng, L. X. and Miao, X. W. (2001). *Contrastive Study of Cohesion in English and Chinese.* Shanghai. Shanghai Foreign Language Teaching and Learning Press.

Zhou, X. (1997) Material and Relational Transitivity Clauses in Mandarin Chinese. Ph.D. Dissertation. The University of Melbourne.

Zhou, X. (1999) The Transitivity System in Material Clauses in Mandarin Chinese. Contemporary Linguistics 1 (3) 36-50. (Chinese Journal)

Appendix

Appendix A: Coding Sheet*

标号：_____

NO:　　_____1_____

　　请仔细阅读每一段叙述，并在下面标出你能在每一段叙述中找到的粗体动词。要求叙述中的动词出现的环境与下面相同或相近。

　　Please read each narrative carefully, and mark out the following blackened verbs which you could find in each narrative. The verbs appear in the narrative should be the same as or similar to as they appear in the following context.

1. 图中**有**两个人（一个男人和一个女人/一个男孩和一个女孩/一对夫妻/一对恋人）。　　　　　　　　　　　　　　(6**)
   There **are** two persons (a boy and a girl / husband and wife / lovers) in the picture.
2. 他们**是**一对恋人（一个男孩和一个女孩/一对夫妻/一对恋人/儿子和母亲）。　　　　　　　　　　　　　　　　　　(5)
   They **are** lovers (a boy and a girl / lovers / husband and wife / son and mom).
3. 一个女孩(一个女的/那个女的/那个女人)指着树上的一个鸟巢。　　(1)
   A girl (a female / the woman / the lady) points to a bird nest in a tree.
4. 在鸟巢里，一只鸟在喂小鸟。　　　　　　　　　　　　　　　(1)

In the nest, a bird is feeding its young.

5. 一个男孩(一个男人)在看。　　　　　　　　　　　　(4)

A boy (a man) looks on.

6. 那个女孩(那个女的/那个女的/那个女人)在看，　　　(4)

While the girl（the female/ the woman/ the lady）is watching,

7. 那个男孩(那个男的/那个男的/那个男人)爬上树，　　(1)

The boy (the male/ the man/ that man) climbs into the tree,

8. 接近(爬向)了鸟巢。　　　　　　　　　　　　　　(1)

and reaches for the nest.

9.（大/老）鸟吓走了。　　　　　　　　　　　　　　(2)

The (big/ old) bird is scared away.

10. 那个男孩(那个男的/那个男的/那个男人)**依**在树枝上。　(4)

The boy (the male/ the man/ that man) is leaning on the branch.

11. 树枝**断**了。　　　　　　　　　　　　　　　　　(1)

The branch **breaks**.

12. 鸟巢和那个男孩(那个男的/那个男的/那个男人)**掉**在地上。　(1)

The nest and the boy (the male/ the man/ that man) **fall** to the ground.

13. 在这过程中，男孩(男的/那个男的/那个男人)**摔断**了腿。　(1)

The boy (the male/ the man/ that man) **breaks** his leg in the process.

14. 那个男孩(那个男的/那个男的/那个男人)**躺**在掉下来的鸟巢附近，(4)

While the boy (the male/ the man/ that man) **lies** near the fallen nest,

15. 那个女孩(那个女的/那个女的/那个女人)到附近**请（寻**求帮助。(3)

the girl（the female/ the women/ the lady）seeks (asks) help from a nearby house.

16. 那个男孩(那个男的/那个男的/那个男人)被用担架**抬**上了救护车。(1)

The boy (the male/ the man/ that man) is carried on a stretcher to an ambulance.

17. 那个男孩(那个男的/那个男的/那个男人)**躺**在医院的床上，腿上打着石膏，　　　　　　　　　　　　　　　　　(4)

The boy (the male/ the man/ that man) is **lying** on a hospital bed with his leg in a cast,

18. 他母亲（那个女孩/那个女的/那个女的/那个女人）悲伤地**看**着他。(4)

   His mother（the girl / the female / the woman / the lady）sadly **looks** on.

19. 鸟妈妈(大鸟/老鸟/母鸟)在外面因为她孩子的死而**哭**。　　　　(4)

   Outside, the mother bird (the big bird / the old bird / the female bird) **cries** over the loss of her young.

* 1 and 2 have been added, 14, 15 and 18 have been modified.

** Code for transitivity.

Appendix B: Examples of Empty "be" Relational Process in Chinese

The typical verb "be" is used in relational process. However, this phenomenon is limited to English; it does not work in some relational processes in Chinese language. For example:

1. 在　树　上 这个　男　　的, (Participant 1)

   In　tree　up　this　male particle,

   This man is in the tree,

2. 鸟雀　在　这　半　　边，(Participant 8)

   Birds　in　this　half　side,

   The birds are in this side,

3. 当然　　　了　这个　鸟雀　在树上, (Participant 13)

   Of course particle　this　bird　in tree up,

   Of course, the bird are in the tree,

4. 老　　鸟　在　边　上。(Participant 13)

   Old　bird　in　side　up.

   The old bird is at the side.

5. 老　　鸟　还　在　那里。(Participant 41)

   Old　bird　still　in　there.

   The old bird is still there.

6. 这　　在　医院 (Participant 43)

   This　in　hospital,

   This is in the hospital,

7. 这　一　窝　鸟雀　在　树　　枝　上。(Participant 49)

   This one nest　bird　in　tree　branch　up.

   The nest of birds is on the tree branch.

8. 鸟　儿　好　好　的　在　树　上(Participant 53)

   Bird particle good good particle in　tree　up,

   The birds in the tree are in good shape,

Verb "be" is not used in the above examples. This means that verb "be" can be unnecessary in relational process in Chinese. Chinese use the following examples in daily life:

9. 他　在　　家。

He　at　home

He is at home.

10. 那　　个　　男　　的　　在　医院.

That　particle　man　particle　at　hospital

That man is at hospital.

In Chinese in 他在家 (*he at home*), the verb *be* (*is*) is not used. So a conclusion is drawn that the verb "be" could not be necessary in Chinese language when the relational process is used to express *circumstantial* relation.

Verb "be" can also be unnecessary in traditional (ancient) Chinese. For example,

11. 君　　君，　臣　　臣，　父　父，　子　子。

Prince prince, minister minister, father father, son son.

Although the verb "be" does not appear in the above example, Chinese can perfectly understand it, and to them, the sentence clearly means that "Let the prince be a prince, the minister a minister, the father a father, and the son a son." Thus, transitivity in SFT needs to be extended to cover the absence of verb "be" in the relational process in Chinese language. In this case, the absence of verb "be" can be called *zero* or *empty* "be" relation.

Appendix C: Abbreviations

SFT: Systemic Functional Theory
GLM: General Linear Model
ANOVA: Analysis of Variance
DOE: Design of Experiments